State of Vermont
Department of Lib...
Northwest Regiona...
RFD #2 Box 10...
Fairfax, VT 05464

VERMONT DEPARTMENT OF LIBRARIES
STATE REGIONAL LIBRARY
BOX 1870
MONTPELIER, VERMONT 05602

WITHDRAWN

SURROGATE MOTHERS

also by Elaine Landau
ALZHEIMER'S DISEASE

SURROGATE MOTHERS

by Elaine Landau

FRANKLIN WATTS
New York/London/Toronto/Sydney/1988

Photographs courtesy of:
Photo Researchers: pp. 18 (Hank Morgan/ Science Source), 20 (Martin Dohrn/IVF Unit, Cromwell Hospital/Science Photo Library); AP/Wide World: pp. 27, 34, 41, 58, 61, 69, 79, 91, 94, 106, 110; UPI/Bettmann Newsphotos: pp. 65, 84, 100.

Library of Congress Cataloging-in-Publication Data

Landau, Elaine.
   Surrogate mothers.
   Bibliography: p.
   Includes index.
   Summary: Examines the moral, ethical, legal, and emotional issues involved in the controversial practice of surrogate motherhood.
   1. Surrogate mothers—United States—Juvenile literature. [1. Surrogate mothers]   I. Title.
HQ759.5.L36   1988   306.8'743   88-5551
ISBN 0-531-10603-9

Copyright © 1988 by Elaine Landau
All rights reserved
Printed in the United States of America
6 5 4 3 2 1

Contents

1
Surrogate Mothers   9

2
Infertility and the New
Birth Technologies   13

3
Surrogate Mothers and the Law   29

4
Portrait of a Surrogate   53

5
Moral and Ethical Issues   67

6
The Case of Baby M   81

**7
Baby M—
Whose Child Is She?** 104

Epilogue 117

Source Notes 119

For Further Reading 123

Index 125

For Marilyn Lubin

1
Surrogate Mothers

Surrogate mother—The term has currently come to describe a woman who conceives, carries, and gives birth to a baby for another person. In most instances, the surrogate mother becomes pregnant through artificial insemination with the sperm of a man whose wife cannot have a baby. She carries the child for nine months, and, after delivering the infant, surrenders it to the couple. The couple will adopt and raise the child. The surrogate will be paid a fee for her services. Sometimes referred to as angels of mercy, other times labeled "mercenary mommies," women who act as surrogate mothers are engaged in one of the most controversial practices in America today.

In his book, *The Surrogate Mother*, Noel P. Keane, an attorney active in the area of surrogate motherhood and adoption, describes perhaps the earliest surrogate mother case to capture national media attention.[1] It took place in 1977 and involved three young people from Detroit, Michigan. Debbie, George, and Sue (actual names) were to become world famous as a result of their actions.

Debbie, the fourth of six children, had always dreamed of having a family of her own, and her husband George had shared her hope. Unfortunately, frequently recurring medical problems had prevented Debbie from conceiving. Nevertheless, she continued to try to become pregnant.

However, late one snowy evening in January 1977, the couple's dream was shattered forever. Debbie had begun to experience severe stomach and abdominal cramps. As the pain continued to worsen, she realized that she was bleeding heavily. Since her husband, George, was still at work, Debbie's closest friend, Sue, insisted on taking her to the hospital.

Debbie was admitted to the hospital, and later a hysterectomy was performed on her. As a result of the surgery, Debbie was unable to have children.

Following her operation, Debbie became extremely despondent and depressed. She told family members that she felt as though an important part of her life was over. Her husband, George, did his best to convince his wife that he had married her because he loved her, not simply to become a father. Still, Debbie proved to be difficult to console, and she was reluctant to abandon her dream of becoming a mother.

Debbie read as much as she could about adoption. She and George applied to the Wayne County Catholic Social Services for a child, but they felt discouraged by their experience at the agency. After being offered an application blank, they were informed that there was a seven-year waiting list. There were already over two thousand applicants ahead of them. The couple began to seriously doubt whether they would ever become parents.

It was Sue who came up with the idea of acting as a surrogate mother for George and Debbie's child. The two women had grown extremely close over the years.

Sue was a single woman in her twenties without children of her own. Debbie had always been there for *her*, Sue felt; now she had found a way in which to help her close friend fulfill a lifelong dream.

Sue, Debbie, and George excitedly contemplated their plan together. If everything went well, Debbie would have a baby in about nine months, instead of waiting seven years.

However, these three young people were not embarking on a clear-cut path, and there were no guidelines for them to follow. Even from the start, they knew that there would be obstacles to overcome as well as important questions to be answered.

Would they be able to find a doctor willing to artificially inseminate Sue with George's sperm? What would each of them tell friends and relatives? And perhaps most importantly, later on, what would the child be told?

As it turned out, after being unable to find a doctor to assist them, Debbie and Sue did the artificial insemination themselves. Assisted only by what they could glean from a book and two sterilized syringes and vials purchased at the local drug store, the women performed the procedure. Since they had kept careful records of Sue's menstrual cycle and charted her daily temperature, they were able to pinpoint Sue's fertile period. After the procedure was over, the three went out to a restaurant to celebrate. Their endeavor proved to be a success. Within weeks, a pregnancy test revealed that Sue was pregnant.

Sue's pregnancy went smoothly. They were able to locate an obstetrician who was more interested in delivering a healthy, normal baby than in passing judgment on the child's surrogate status. The three also secured the services of Noel P. Keane to act as their attorney in arranging for Debbie's legal adoption of the infant. Since that time, Mr. Keane has become one of the best-known attorneys in the surrogate parenting field.

In August, when Sue was nearly three months pregnant, she and Debbie and George, along with Mr. Keane, were invited to appear on "The Phil Donahue Show." On the day of their appearance, the television studio's auditorium was filled to capacity. Although many audience members and call-in viewers expressed their doubts about surrogate motherhood, countless others were excited at the prospect.

The case of Sue, Debbie, and George is unusual. There was never a legal contract drawn up between Debbie and George as the adoptive parents and Sue as the surrogate mother. Their entire agreement was based on love, friendship, and trust. As none of them believed in abortion, it was decided that there could be no turning back once the child was conceived. Debbie also insisted that if—at any point during the pregnancy—Sue changed her mind about keeping the baby, the child would be hers. Debbie and George also decided that when the child was old enough to understand, he or she would learn the truth. Sue had a difficult labor, but eventually the baby was born, and Debbie became a mother.

As Debbie gazed down at the baby for the first time, she could scarcely believe her eyes. She felt as though her little girl was the most beautiful and wonderful child she'd ever seen. The miracle of birth had touched Debbie's life—a miracle which she once thought she'd never experience.

This early instance of surrogate motherhood, arrived at through an agreement between close friends, had a happy ending. Since that time, however, the use of surrogate mothers has burgeoned into a thriving commercial enterprise often involving many diverse individuals with varied motives and financial interests. The repercussions of surrogate agreements are often complex and multifaceted as the process raises difficult societal issues.

2
Infertility and the New Birth Technologies

Although Lynn and Raymond married when both were twenty-seven, they had firmly decided to postpone having children until they were in their thirties. At the time, the couple had based their decision on what had seemed to them to be sound reasons.

When they were first married, Raymond had held down a full-time job while attending evening classes to complete his doctoral degree in chemistry. Raymond spent most weeknight evenings in class or at the university's lab, while his weekends were largely devoted to developing advanced research proposals.

At that point in Raymond's life, there was little time left over for relaxation or recreation, let alone parenting. Raymond loved children and had always wanted a family, but it was important to him that he have ample time to devote to a child. He felt that it would be unfair to a baby, to Lynn, and to himself to become a father before he felt ready.

Lynn also had important career goals of her own

which she wished to pursue. She had been fortunate in landing a junior executive position with a prestigious New York advertising firm. As assistant to one of the company's most influential vice presidents, she knew that if she worked hard and used her talents well, she'd be certain to rise within the company's hierarchy. Although Lynn planned to eventually take some time off to raise a family, she did not want to stop working until she had attained a senior position with a comfortable salary.

Another reason why the couple chose to wait to have children had to do with their incomes. Both wanted their children to be born into a secure financial situation. And despite the fact that it was difficult to put aside very much money while Raymond still paid tuition and Lynn's salary was relatively low, by the time the couple was thirty-five, they had managed to place a down payment on a spacious and attractive home.

Following years of work and preparation, Lynn and Raymond had set the stage for raising their own family. Unfortunately, things didn't work out as Lynn and Raymond had hoped. Close to a year later, Lynn was still not pregnant. Already discouraged and filled with self-doubt, Lynn and Raymond sought the help of a fertility specialist.

Infertility, which often results from a medical problem, can trigger emotional havoc, both within individuals and between spouses. Throughout history, women have been traditionally blamed for infertility, although the man is just as likely to be responsible. History is replete with instances of kings who abandoned their wives because the woman in question had not produced an heir to the throne.

Even today, coming to grips with infertility can be extremely distressing for some women. Regardless of whether the woman is a homemaker or a career woman, it is always unsettling to learn that you're unable to have children.

Many men also find it disconcerting to deal with the reality that they are unable to impregnate their wives. Some may regard the ability to reproduce as a reflection of their sexuality and manliness. Unfortunately, in a "macho society," a sterile male may too often find himself the object of ridicule rather than compassion.

Often, infertility counselors who have worked with couples unable to have children say that many of their clients also experience a profound sense of loss. Accepting one's infertility may be a bit like contending with the loss of a loved one; in a sense, couples mourn the death of the baby who never was.

RESOLVE is a national self-help group for those who are infertile. In this organization, individuals and couples are able to come together to discuss their common problem. There are currently forty-three RESOLVE chapters across America. At RESOLVE meetings, members may hear professionals speak on the causes and ramifications of infertility, or may simply discuss what's happened to them. One woman at a RESOLVE meeting described her reaction to learning that she was infertile.

> *Once you find out that you're never going to have the children you've always planned on having, your reaction to other people's children around you changes. Now whenever I see a cute toddler in the supermarket, I start to imagine what it would be like to be his or her mother. I used to love to be near my friends who were pregnant or the ones who had recently had babies. I wanted to learn as much as I could to prepare myself for the birth of my own baby. But now I stay away from those situations whenever I can. At this point, I can't even hug their kids without starting to cry.*
>
> *It's hard to pass a toy store, a playground, or even*

a children's furniture or clothing shop. Lately, everything seems to remind me of what I've missed out on. I've even avoided seeing my parents lately. I'm their only offspring and I know how badly they've wanted grandchildren. I just can't bear to face them yet.

The process of learning that one or both partners is infertile can be difficult and complicated as well. Often couples feel as though sex has been turned from a spontaneous expression of love into a precisely timed act distantly choreographed by a physician to result in a pregnancy.

Keeping records of the woman's daily temperature and the number of times the couple had sex during the month may be required. A couple may undergo batteries of tests, as well as various treatments to increase their chances of having a baby. Many individuals have undergone frequent examinations, taken medications, and had surgery. Emotional pressures may build within the marriage, but many couples will continue to try. Unfortunately, the various drugs and fertility treatments aren't always successful for everyone. Some couples will eventually face the fact that they will never be able to have children biologically.

Some fertile couples who wish to have children may choose not to become biological parents. These are individuals who have sought genetic counseling and have learned that either the husband or wife or both might pass on a serious genetic disorder to the child. Recent advances in the field of genetics have helped to allow doctors to predict whether these couples can have a healthy child. Today many gynecologists and obstetricians, as well as specialists in medical genetics, have begun to offer genetic information and testing to prospective parents.

Couples who can most benefit from genetic counseling are those in which one or both partners has a genetic abnormality or disease; couples who have already had a child with a genetic defect; or couples in which the woman is over thirty-five and is therefore more likely to give birth to a child with chromosomal abnormalities.

In addition, various ethnic groups may be more prone to certain diseases. For example, one hereditary disorder that often affects individuals of Eastern European Jewish origin is known as Tay-Sachs disease. As Tay-Sachs is caused by a recessive defective gene, an individual with the Tay-Sachs trait may appear normal and in good health. However, problems can arise if two people with the Tay-Sachs trait decide to marry and have a family. The odds are one in four that a child born to them will have Tay-Sachs disease.

Couples handle the results of genetic counseling and testing in different ways. Some may so badly want a child that they proceed with the pregnancy, hoping to defy the odds. Individuals who are not morally opposed to abortion may allow conception to occur and later undergo a medical test called *amniocentesis*. Through amniocentesis, it is possible to determine if certain genetic disorders, such as Tay-Sachs, have affected the fetus. If, at this point, the couple learns that their child will be afflicted, they may elect to abort the fetus.

However, for many individuals, the knowledge that they are capable of passing on a serious disorder to their offspring presents a serious dilemma. Although the prospect of aborting the child they've dreamed about for so long is unacceptable, they are just as reluctant to inflict the pain and suffering of a serious illness on their baby.

Couples who decide not to procreate because of a potential genetic problem often experience many of the same emotions felt by infertile couples. At various times, they may feel isolated, defective as human beings, and exceedingly jealous of couples with healthy babies. In

Couples who discover, through genetic counseling, that they cannot have children handle their dilemma in various ways. Some resort to the new reproductive technologies.

some cases, they may mourn the end of their family's bloodline.

Once couples have given up on the possibility of biological conception, they may turn to other options. In the past, adoption was considered a viable alternative for childless couples. Homeless children were provided with parents and a home, and couples without children were finally able to enjoy raising a family.

However, adopting a normal healthy infant today is not as easy as it was some years ago. This decline may be partially due to the widespread use of contraceptives and the availability of safe legal abortion in the United States. Social attitudes toward unwed mothers in some areas have relaxed as well. As a result, it is now not uncommon for unmarried women to keep their babies rather than place them for adoption.

Couples who contact an adoption agency may soon learn that adopting a baby is not a quick or simple procedure. Often couples may find themselves faced with a barrage of regulations and standards to which they are unable to conform. Frequently, couples may be told that they are too old or that they haven't been married long enough to be considered good candidates for adoptive parents. One adoption agency discouraged a couple from applying because the husband and wife were of different faiths. Another agency did not approve of a woman who had been working full time and had indicated that she planned to remain at her job once she and her husband had adopted a baby.

In addition, adoption procedures generally entail a good deal of red tape as well as an extremely thorough investigation into the lives of the prospective parents. The costs involved in adopting a baby can also amount to several thousand dollars.

Some individuals and couples—those who are unable to biologically reproduce, those who run the risk of transmitting genetic conditions, those who have ruled out or been turned down for adoption—may choose to remain childless. However, still other couples have refused to give up their dream of having children. In some instances, individuals have been willing to try every technologically advanced method of conception and childbearing publicly available, if it seems suitable for them. These newer options are described below.

IN VITRO FERTILIZATION (IVF)

In in vitro fertilization, a physician surgically removes an egg from a woman's ovary. The doctor then places

Prepared petri dishes containing unfertilized human eggs, prior to being mixed with human sperm

the egg in a small, shallow, loosely covered container called a petri dish. Some of the husband's sperm is then added to the petri dish in order to fertilize the egg. Once the egg has been fertilized, it must be placed in the woman's uterus. To accomplish this process, the doctor will use a long tube that passes through the woman's vagina into the uterus.

If all goes well, the fertilized egg will implant in the woman's uterus, where it will grow and develop as would any biologically conceived child. Although children whose birth resulted from in vitro fertilization have often been referred to in the media as "test-tube babies," the image evoked by that label is quite misleading. None of these children ever developed in an oversized test tube for nine months.

The most likely candidate for the IVF procedure is a women whose Fallopian tubes have been blocked or damaged. The Fallopian tubes are the slender pair of ducts that carry the egg from the ovary to the uterus. Tubal problems in women may most commonly result from abdominal surgery, complications resulting from a contraceptive device known as the IUD, or a sexually transmitted disease. An infection in that area can also scar the tubes, stopping the passage of the fertilized egg or causing adhesions that may block or close either end of the Fallopian tube.

It's been estimated that approximately 490,000 infertile women in the United States alone suffer from the problems described above.[1] However, these women still might be able to have a baby through in vitro fertilization. In vitro fertilization can also prove beneficial to women who have changed their minds after having undergone some forms of voluntary sterilization.

A number of clinics have also made in vitro fertilization available to couples in whom the woman's tubes may be normal, but where the male involved has a low sperm count. Even though it only takes one sperm to fertilize a woman's egg, it is estimated that at least ten million sperm must be released into the woman's body. However, with IVF, a man does not need a sperm count of ten million or more, since the sperm is put in direct contact with the egg. Having eliminated the need for the sperm to travel through the woman's vagina, cervix, and uterus to the Fallopian tubes for fertilization to occur allows the male with a significantly lower sperm count to still have a child that is genetically his.

The first IVF baby, Louise Brown, was born in England in 1978. Although today there are dozens of clinics across America that offer IVF, there are still many more couples desiring the procedure than may be accommodated. In addition, not everyone who wishes to try IVF may be considered medically suitable for the process. Most clinics demand that prospective candidates for the procedure meet specific medical guidelines.

The medical expenses associated with in vitro fertilization are quite high. And, as at this time, IVF costs are not covered by any form of health insurance, the full monetary burden falls on the couple. The cost to the couple averages between $4,000 and $5,000 for each attempt made at IVF, and generally the procedure must be tried a number of times before it is successful.

Some clinics insist that all couples accepted for the procedure sign a contract agreeing to undergo a minimum of four IVF attempts. However, the cost remains the same each time, and regardless of how many times a couple undergoes IVF, there is still no guarantee that their efforts will result in the birth of a child.

Couples who can afford the time and money involved in repeated attempts at IVF must be aware that even under the best of circumstances, IVF has an extremely low success rate. Many things can go wrong at various stages of the procedure. The egg may not be fertilized, a fertilized egg may not implant well, or the embryo may abort itself before the woman even knows she's pregnant. In many instances, miscarriages have occurred later on in the pregnancy.

In 1980, it was reported at a world conference on IVF that although in vitro fertilization had been attempted on more than twenty thousand women at that point, only three proven births had actually occurred. However, within recent years, the success rate, although still relatively low, has dramatically improved. This has been largely due to improvements in IVF techniques. The American Fertility Society now indicates that the success rate for in vitro fertilization ranges between ten and twenty percent; this means that one or two women out of every ten who try the procedure will actually give birth to a baby.[2]

ARTIFICIAL INSEMINATION BY DONOR (AID)

Artificial insemination by donor, or AID, is a process used by couples when the male is infertile. AID may also be selected by couples in which the male has the potential to pass on a genetic defect. In addition, single women without male partners may turn to AID as a way to have children.

The procedure is commonly employed in the United States today. In fact, ten to twenty thousand American children are born as a result of the process each year, and the procedure has a fifty-seven percent national success rate.[3]

With AID, a woman will visit her doctor's office a day prior to ovulation. The doctor will insert sperm from an anonymous donor into the woman. The semen will either be squirted directly into the vagina against the cervix or placed in a small cap that is put over the woman's cervix. At times, AID has also been completed without medical assistance.

AID is painless. After insemination, the woman remains in a reclining position for about thirty minutes to allow the sperm to travel to her Fallopian tubes. If the doctor used a cervical cap for the insemination, the cap should remain in place for approximately six hours.

It is extremely crucial that individuals desiring the AID procedure be certain of their physician's assurance that all potential sperm donors have been screened for venereal disease (including the HLV virus, which can lead to acquired immune deficiency syndrome—AIDS) and genetic disorders; these may be unintentionally passed on through artificial insemination by donor. It is also important that a reputable sperm bank be used.

SURROGATE MOTHERS

Generally, a surrogate mother is a woman who is artificially inseminated with the sperm of a man whose spouse is incapable of biologically having a baby. The surrogate carries the child for nine months and, after its delivery, permits the couple for whom she performed the service to adopt the infant. At times, single women have used the services of surrogate mothers as well.

Surrogacy may be viewed by some as being more problematic than other forms of the new reproductive technology. For example, IVF may involve just the married couple, while in AID, the third party simply donates germinal material. But only surrogate parenting involves the third party in the lengthy and intimate act of carrying a baby for nine months.

One surrogate mother has referred to herself as a human incubator. The baby will genetically be the product of the surrogate mother and the male partner of the couple. The child will probably resemble them both. That is why most couples seek out a surrogate mother who physically resembles the adoptive mother.

Today, surrogate mothers may be considered an alternative for infertile women. In fact, advanced medical technology is even beginning to make it possible for a new type of surrogate mother to exist. One such method is called embryo transfer. In this manner, a woman who is still capable of producing healthy eggs, but cannot bear a child, could have one or more of her eggs surgically removed and fertilized outside her body by her husband's sperm through the in vitro fertilization process. However, instead of having the fertilized egg reinserted into her body to develop and grow, the egg would instead be placed in the body of a surrogate who'd be capable of carrying the baby to term.

The baby would not be genetically connected to the surrogate in any way. After the baby's birth, the genetic parents who supplied both the egg and the sperm would bring up their own child.

In Johannesburg, South Africa, Pat Anthony, a forty-eight-year-old grandmother acted in this capacity for her own daughter. Karen Ferreira-Jorge had nearly died two years earlier, giving birth to her first child. As a result of complications, her doctors had had to remove Ms. Ferreira-Jorge's uterus, leaving her biologically incapable of giving birth again.

Ms. Ferreira-Jorge and her husband, Alcino, desperately wanted more children. They had contemplated adoption and even hiring a surrogate mother. But Karen's mother, Pat, feared that an outsider might eventually want to keep the baby. Therefore, she volunteered to act as a surrogate mother for her daughter and son-in-law.

To medically start the procedure, daughter Karen was given drugs to stimulate her ovaries. Later on, the infertility specialists at Johannesburg's Park Lane Clinic removed eleven of Karen's eggs. The eggs were combined with Alcino's sperm through in vitro fertilization. Two days later, four fertilized eggs were surgically implanted in Pat Anthony's uterus.

Initially, the physicians involved seriously doubted the successful outcome of this endeavor. They felt that Pat's age was against her. Yet within weeks, it was discovered that not only had Ms. Anthony become pregnant, but that she was going to have triplets.

Ms. Anthony gave birth to the triplets by Caesarian section in October 1987. There were two boys and a girl, named David, Jose, and Paula.

Even though Pat Anthony had carried the babies to term, she claimed that she still felt as though she were their grandmother rather than their mother. She explained that her body had merely been a vessel through which her own daughter might be given a family. As Ms. Anthony told *People*, "Even two days before the birth, I can feel them kicking inside me and I just laugh. I don't feel any strong maternal instincts or urges. I am doing this because my daughter, not me, was desperate for children and unhappy for it."[4]

With the birth of David, Jose, and Paula, Pat Anthony became the first woman to give birth to her own grandchildren, as well as the first surrogate mother to produce in vitro or test-tube triplets.

Another variation of this method is known as surrogate embryo transfer. Here a baby is born as a result of using a surrogate's egg fertilized by the husband's sperm. This method is helpful to women who are able to carry a baby to term, but are unable to produce the egg needed for conception. Such women may have prematurely begun menopause, been born without the biological ability to produce eggs, or may have had to have their ovaries removed surgically. Some women who are able to produce eggs may even consider this alternative if it becomes widely available, in instances where the possibility of passing on a genetic defect to a biologically conceived child exists.

In February 1984, the world's first surrogate embryo transfer baby was born. Wearing lapel buttons bearing the slogan, "IT'S A BOY," Los Angeles physicians proudly proclaimed a medical first—a healthy infant who had been conceived by one woman had been born through another woman's body.

The woman who gave birth to the child was a Los Angeles resident in her thirties who had unsuccessfully attempted to conceive a child for more than ten years. Then she tried surrogate embryo transfer.

The surrogate who donated the egg had been artificially inseminated with sperm from the woman's husband. After about five days following fertilization, the donor woman's uterus was *lavaged,* or washed out. The embryo was recovered from the lavage fluid and then transferred to the recipient's uterus.

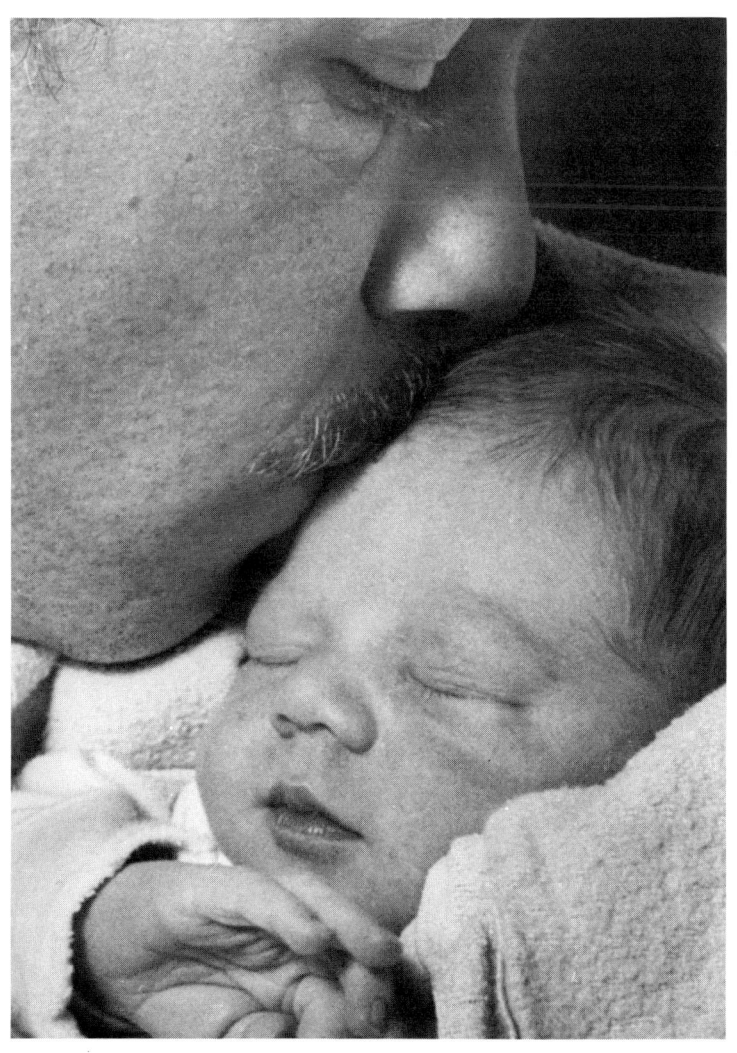

*Travis Cody McCullar,
the second baby in the
United States born from a
frozen embryo implant pregnancy.
The frozen embryos were
transferred into the mother.*

Following the birth, the new mother said: "It's just a miracle. The miracle is not that I've given birth, but that someone else's egg has grown inside my body."[5] As research in this area continues, the process of surrogate embryo transfer is expected to become a medical reality for large numbers of women. However, in this procedure it is important to note that the baby is genetically linked to the father and the surrogate who donated the egg, and as a result may physically resemble them both.

EGG DONATION

Still another form of surrogate motherhood, similar to surrogate embryo transfer, is known as egg donation. Egg donation would also be helpful to women who are able to carry a baby to term, but are unable to produce the egg needed for conception.

The procedure of egg donation has already been accomplished in Melbourne, Australia, and is currently being further explored by scientists in Europe. In egg donation, an egg is surgically extracted from the ovary of a woman donor or surrogate. The egg is then surgically inserted into the lower portion of the Fallopian tube of the woman wishing to have the baby. The woman receiving the egg can then attempt to become pregnant either through sexual intercourse or artificial insemination.

Once the egg becomes fertilized, the baby develops normally. Although the baby will be raised by the father and the woman who received the egg and carried the baby to term, as in surrogate embryo transfer, the child's genetic mother is the woman who donated the egg.

These are only a sample of the alternatives to naturally conceiving and giving birth to a baby that may involve a surrogate and advanced technology. Research in this area has continued to grow, and in the not too distant future, even more dramatic and innovative alternatives may be available as well.

3
Surrogate Mothers and the Law

As the use of surrogate mothers has become more commonplace, a good deal of public attention has been focused on the legal ramifications involved in these types of relationships. Most couples who seek a surrogate mother to bear a child for them are assisted by an attorney. For the couple's legal protection, the attorney will draw up a contract outlining the duties and responsibilities of all parties involved. In some instances, the attorney may even help to locate a woman to serve as a surrogate.

The surrogate contract is generally deemed necessary to help ensure that the infant will be surrendered to the couple immediately following its birth and that the adoption will proceed smoothly. A contract is also valuable to the surrogate mother, to legally guarantee that both her fee and her medical expenses will be paid according to the agreement.

Surrogate mother contracts generally list the parties' obligations to one another. A typical contract calls for the woman acting as the surrogate mother to be artificially inseminated with the sperm of the male member of the couple. If the surrogate becomes pregnant and delivers a baby, she is to turn it over to the couple who originally contracted her services. The contract will also outline the couple's obligation to pay all of the surrogate's medical bills as well as any other pregnancy-related expenses incurred by her while carrying the baby. Most contracts also specify that if the child is born with any form of birth defect, the prospective parents are still obligated to take the child and to pay all related expenses.

In addition, the contract will require that the couple put the surrogate's fee in an escrow account. This account will be administered by the attorney, who will pay the surrogate's fee once she has fulfilled the terms of the contract. In the past, the standard fee paid to a surrogate mother was approximately ten thousand dollars, although recently substantially higher fees have been reported.

If the surrogate mother has a miscarriage, she will usually be guaranteed at least partial payment of her fee. The amount she receives will vary according to the number of months she carried the child. In return, the surrogate's obligation generally entails seeing an obstetrician regularly, as well as avoiding illegal and nonprescription drugs, alcohol, and cigarettes.

Besides the contract existing between the couple and the surrogate mother, many attorneys who handle surrogate situations also insist on a contract between themselves and their clients, the couple. This contract largely exists for the lawyer's own protection. It will usually state that the lawyer is not responsible for guaranteeing that a pregnancy will occur, or that the surrogate will abide by the terms of her contract. In instances in which the above situations occur, the attorney's legal fees are generally still not reduced or refunded.

Some countries have already passed strict bans against profit-making surrogacy. In Britain, the Surrogacy Arrangements Act of 1985 makes it a criminal offense for third parties to benefit from commercial surrogacy.[1] Under the Act, a surrogate mother is defined as a woman who carries a child in pursuance of a prior agreement with the intent of handing over the child after its birth to another person or persons with the understanding that she will receive payment.

Payment is defined as either money or money's worth, in order to prevent transferring material goods to the surrogate mother as a means of circumventing the law's intent. The Act also prohibits advertising in connection with commercial surrogacy.

In the Australian state of Victoria, the government has also set firm limits on the new reproductive technologies. The Victorian legislation makes it an offense punishable by up to two years in prison to give or receive a payment for acting as a surrogate mother. It is also illegal to publish any advertisement seeking a surrogate.

In February 1988, in the state of New Jersey, surrogate motherhood for a fee was declared illegal. But there are still no laws to protect any of the parties involved in these agreements. Surrogate mothers currently exist in a state of limbo. For thousands of childless individuals who yearn to be parents, advanced technology for new methods and forms of conception cannot be developed quickly enough. But although the procedures have raised the hopes of millions, the technology also raises countless legal questions and problems as well.

Alexander Morgan Capron—the Norman Topping Professor of Law, Medicine and Public Policy at the University of Southern California—testified concerning these issues before a House of Representatives science subcommittee as early as August 1984. "Many of the new reproductive possibilities remain so novel that the terms are lacking to describe the human relationships they can create. For example, what does one call a woman who bears a child conceived from another woman's egg? I'm not even sure we know what to call the area under inquiry."

While new techniques of fertilization are becoming almost commonplace, federal laws designed to guard against the dangers of exploitation and manipulation are nearly nonexistent. Many of the state and local laws regarding paternity questions seem outdated and illogical when applied to today's surrogate mother situations.

As Doris J. Freed, of the American Bar Association's family law section committee, told *Time* magazine: "It's going to take years of debate, legislation, trial and error to figure out how to deal with these problems."[2] Perhaps the dilemma was best summed up by University of Maryland philosophy professor Samuel Gorovitz, when he told a House subcommittee that "we have a patchwork of laws and gaps, stigmas, deprivations, uncertainties, confusions, and fears."

For example, artificial insemination by donor has been widely practiced since the 1960s. Although over 250,000 births have resulted from the procedure, the law still lags far behind. For example, in 1963 a New York court ruled that a child born by AID (artificial insemination by donor) was illegitimate, despite the fact that the woman's husband may have wanted the child and consented to the procedure. Another New York court hearing a similar case, in 1973, came to the opposite conclusion. Today, twenty-nine states, including New York, have legislated that babies born as a result of artificial insemination by donor are the legitimate offspring of the mother and her husband, provided that the husband consented to the procedure.

However, in the remaining states, the paternity question is still unsettled. If a couple with a child conceived through AID divorce, can the father refuse to pay child support on the grounds that the child is not his, although he may have initially agreed to having a child in that manner? On the other hand, can a woman deny her ex-husband visitation rights on the same grounds?

There are also no specific laws to deal with the legal ramifications of in vitro fertilization (IVF). However, following the United States 1973 Supreme Court decision legalizing abortion, a number of states passed laws to prohibit or limit any form of "experimentation" with fetuses. Doctors in some of those areas hesitate to perform the IVF process for fear of being prosecuted under the law, despite the fact that the procedure is not specifically mentioned.

The new methods of fertilization and conception have created a confusing maze of legal questions, in the United States and abroad. Few countries are prepared to deal with the potential dilemmas they present. One such striking illustration occurred in France and involved the case of Corinne Parpalaix, a twenty-two-year-old secretary who worked for a French police department in Marseille.

Mrs. Parpalaix had been recently widowed. Her husband had died of cancer the preceding year, but before his death, he had deposited semen in a sperm bank. Now Mrs. Parpalaix wished to be artificially inseminated with her late husband's sperm, so that she could continue his family line. However, the sperm bank officials refused to comply with her request on the grounds that her husband had left no instructions as to what he wanted done with the sperm.

The widow took her case to court. Traditional French law offered little guidance and few precedents on the issue. The French court had to determine the legal status of the dead man's sperm. Could it be viewed as an organ transplant of sorts? Is frozen sperm as inheritable as any piece of property might be?

Corinne Parpalaix (center), the widow who wanted to be artificially inseminated with her late husband's sperm took her case to a French court when a clinic refused to comply with her request. Her husband had deposited semen in a sperm bank.

The state prosecutor sided with the sperm bank. He argued that the sperm was part of the man's body, despite the fact that the man had been buried over a year ago, while his sperm remained deposited in the sperm bank. The prosecutor stressed that the deceased had a basic right to his body's "physical integrity," or for it to be left intact after death. What he actually meant was that the dead man's widow had no more right to his sperm than she had to his fingers or toes.

The widow's lawyer argued that having placed the sperm in a sperm bank to begin with implied an existing contract between the husband and wife for the sperm's future use. The court ruled in the widow's favor, stating that this "secretion containing the seeds of life" should be given to her. Mrs. Parpalaix told the press this about her future child: "I'll call him Thomas. He'll be a pianist. That's what his father wanted."

The case of an American couple also raises serious questions about the new reproductive technologies, in this case, unused frozen embryos. Mario and Elsa Rios, an affluent American couple, had both had children from former marriages, but they were unable to conceive a child together.

Having gone through various infertility programs, in 1981 they sought the assistance of the research pioneers at the Queen Victoria Medical Center in Melbourne, Australia. At the center, three of Mrs. Rios's egg cells were successfully removed from her body and fertilized with the sperm of an anonymous donor.

At that point, one of the three live embryos was implanted in Mrs. Rios's womb. The remaining two were frozen in order to preserve them for potential later use. In the event that the first transplanted embryo aborted, the remaining two embryos could then be used for future implantation.

Unfortunately, the implanted embryo did spontaneously abort after about ten days. Since at that time

Mrs. Rios indicated that she was not emotionally ready to have the second embryo implanted, the remaining two live embryos were left in their frozen state.

In the ensuing months, the Rioses went to South America, where they adopted a child. Then in the early spring of 1983, both Mario and Elsa Rios, along with their adopted offspring, were killed when their private plane crashed.[3]

Their death raised a host of legal and ethical questions. Now that the Rioses were dead, who should determine the fate of the remaining frozen embryos? Who should inherit the considerable assets of the Rios estate?

Common law tradition in both Australia and the United States has long permitted those who have been conceived but are not yet born to inherit property. But, in the Rios case, although the embryos are alive, the children will never be born unless they are removed from their frozen state and implanted in a woman's womb. The question will not remain a viable issue indefinitely, however, since frozen embryos deteriorate over time and at a point can no longer survive implantation.

A committee convened to decide what should be done with the Rioses' embryos recommended that they be destroyed. However, the state of Victoria legislators rejected the committee's suggestion. Instead, they passed an amendment to a subsequent bill that proposed that the embryos be implanted in surrogate mothers. If the pregnancies were successful and the children born, they could then be placed for adoption. At this time, there has been no further word on whether the embryos were actually implanted.

Reproductive technology involving the use of frozen embryos and the possible complications resulting from it poses unsettling concerns for many. The freezing of sperm and embryos was an important development in the new reproductive technologies. Freezing made the procedures safer and raised the success rate, but it also led to commercialization.

Surrogate mothers currently pose numerous legal dilemmas as well. Although the process is thought of as existing primarily for married couples who are unable to have a baby, should a single woman who wishes to raise a child have legal access to surrogate mothers as well? Some people have questioned the wisdom of making surrogate mother services available to lesbians, transsexuals, and male homosexuals who are unable to procreate, but may desire children of their own. Others insist that the rights of these individuals should not be curtailed because of their sexual orientation. They point to the fact that there is no tangible scientific data to show that children raised in homosexual environments are any less well adjusted than children brought up in heterosexual homes.

The legal rights of a child born as a result of the new methods of conception also need to be legally defined and established. For example, does that child have the right to know its biological parents? Does a child conceived as the result of AID, or through a surrogate mother, have the right to inherit the property of his or her biological parents?

Only recently have a handful of cases been tested in court, and it is highly likely that any decisions arrived at will be subsequently appealed. In the meantime, numerous bills on surrogacy have been introduced and debated in state legislatures across America. The National Committee on Adoption reported that in 1987, twenty-two bills on surrogacy were introduced in sixteen states and the District of Columbia, nine of which seek to outlaw the practice. No final decisions have yet been arrived at. Courts and government commissions in the United States continue to examine whether surrogate mother contracts should be permitted.

As a result, no contract between a surrogate mother

and a couple can be legally binding. Due to the fact that surrogate contracts are not enforceable by law, a number of things can go wrong. For example, even though the contract may specifically prohibit the surrogate mother from drinking alcohol or taking drugs, she may do so anyway. Since very few surrogate mothers actually move in with the child's prospective parents, the couple must rely on the surrogate's integrity to ensure that she will act in the child's best interest. Unfortunately, not all women who have volunteered as surrogates have behaved responsibly with regard to the fetus's well being.

Although some surrogates have adhered to their contracts, others have been unscrupulously dishonest in their dealings with the child's prospective parents. Some have attempted to exhort payments and gifts that far exceeded the originally determined fee. One such surrogate, who had initially agreed to a $10,000 payment, forced the baby's prospective parents to buy her a new car and a fur jacket and to pay off the remaining mortgage on her home. She told the husband and wife that if they failed to meet her demands, she was prepared to have an abortion. The couple, who at this point were desperate for a child, complied with her requests, even though it drained them of nearly all they owned.

The child's father explained their reasons for acting as they did this way.

> *There was really nothing else which we felt we could do. We were at her mercy. I had put my hand on her stomach and felt my baby move. It was alive, it was mine, and my wife and I already loved it. We couldn't allow her to murder our only child.*
>
> *I admit that it was as if we'd paid ransom to her for the baby, but we'd have done anything for that kid. We knew that we'd always be able to make more money*

if we worked hard enough, but there was no way that my wife and I could ever have a baby together. We always said that we'd give everything we had for a child, but I never dreamed that we'd really actually have to.

It is important to remember that two parties are involved in the agreement, and that it may not always be the surrogate mother who fails to comply with the contract's intent. In 1982, Judy Stiver, a twenty-six-year-old clerk from Lansing, Michigan, volunteered to become a surrogate mother. She and her husband, Ray, already had a two-year-old daughter of their own and thought that this might be a good way to earn some needed extra money.

But, unfortunately, the infant son Ms. Stiver gave birth to on January 10, 1983, was a microcephalic baby. This meant that the infant's head was disproportionately small for its body. Usually, microcephalic children are mentally retarded.

Judy Stiver claimed that the child belonged to Alexander Malahoff, a forty-six-year-old accountant from Queens, New York, with whose sperm she had been artificially inseminated. The Malahoffs had turned to a surrogate mother because Nadja, Malahoff's thirty-two-year-old wife, had been unable to have a child. However, at the time of the infant's birth, Alexander Malahoff was separated from his wife. He had hoped the baby would reunite them and help preserve their marriage.

Alexander Malahoff had agreed to pay Judy Stiver $10,000 to act as the surrogate mother. In addition, he was responsible for the total medical costs involved throughout the pregnancy as well as for the actual birth. The legal expenses for the contracted service amounted to $5,000, and there was an additional $1,800 for the artificial insemination process.

Following the infant's birth, Alexander Malahoff

claimed that the baby was not his, but was, in fact, the son of Ray Stiver, the surrogate mother's husband. The Stivers denied Malahoff's charge, stating that they had not had sexual intercourse for thirty days following the insemination, as had been agreed to. Judy Stiver insisted that she had only become pregnant because she was acting in a surrogate capacity. Her sole purpose had been to have a baby for the Malahoffs. She and her husband did not wish to have any more children.

A human leukocyte antigen (HLA) blood test was performed on the infant. This recently developed blood test is regarded as being approximately 99 percent accurate in determining paternity. The blood typing showed that the baby had O positive blood, like that of his mother; Malahoff had AB positive, a type unlikely to produce an O positive child.

As a result of the test, Malahoff refused to accept the child. He returned to New York alone, leaving the baby he had contracted for in Michigan. Before very long, the state of Michigan, acting on the hospital's behalf, served Malahoff with a court order to return to the state for a custody hearing. Malahoff countered this action with a $50 million dollar breach-of-contract suit against the Stivers.

Meanwhile, the child was placed in the care of local social service workers. At times, Judy Stiver was chided by some in the media for not displaying more maternal concern over the fate of her infant. Yet surrogate mothers are usually encouraged to emotionally distance themselves from these children, in order to ease the baby's surrender to the prospective parents.

Soon afterwards, the Stivers announced that they wished to take the baby home, unless it was medically determined that hospitalization or institutionalization was required for the child. When the couple was questioned by reporters as to whether they felt satisfied that Mr. Stiver was the baby's biological father, they admitted

Surrogate mother Judy Stiver, and her husband Ray, left, with Alexander Malahoff, who had contracted with the Stivers for a baby. It was later shown that the baby was probably fathered by Ray Stiver, not Malahoff.

the possibility. Mrs. Stiver added that although she thought that they had abstained from having sexual relations during the required time period, she admitted, "I don't write down every time we have intercourse."

The Stiver–Malahoff case had an obvious solution, because the child's paternity had been wrongly assumed. However, what will happen in the future if prospective parents attempt to reject deformed or sick babies who are the actual offspring of the father involved? Although most surrogacy contracts require that they accept and raise the child, it has already been shown that these contracts are not always enforceable. Although there was nearly positive proof that Alexander Malahoff was not the father of Judy Stiver's baby, in some instances, a blood test may not be totally conclusive in determining paternity.

Even in biologically "correct" surrogate situations, either party may experience a sincere change of heart. At times, prospective parents may have separated or divorced during the contractual period. In such instances, their desire to have a child often seems to end with their marriage.

Other things can go wrong as well. One couple in which an infertile wife claimed that she had always wanted to be a mother contracted for the services of a surrogate mother. Then, in the surrogate's seventh month of pregnancy, the prospective mother suffered a serious nervous collapse and had to be admitted to a mental hospital.

Although she was released shortly after the baby's birth, her doctor warned that it would be inadvisable for her to have to cope with caring for a newborn baby. In cases like these, the babies are often put up for adoption. But if the surrogate mother adhered to her part of the bargain, should she still receive her fee despite the fact that the couple may have voluntarily forfeited their claim to the baby?

Some couples have attempted to withhold payment on the grounds that they never actually proceeded with a legal adoption of the child. At times, surrogate mothers who lacked the funds or resources to secure competent legal assistance for themselves had to go along with the couple's decision to reject the child. Some simply felt forced to put their baby up for adoption, as they were not in a position to raise the child themselves.

While it is true that some prospective parents have gone back on their commitments, in breached surrogate contracts it is more often the surrogate mother who has decided that she wishes to keep her baby. As one surrogate mother explained:

> *It's one thing to sit in a lawyer's office and to sign a contract agreeing to be paid to have a baby and give it up. But once you've carried that child, felt it move and kick in your womb, and gone through the pain of childbirth to give it life, somehow everything changes. That baby is your own flesh and blood. You just can't sell a piece of your soul for the price of a cheap car. Or for any price for that matter. The situation becomes very complicated. After you've bonded with your own baby, you feel very differently than you felt in the lawyer's office when you first signed the contract.*

Custody battles have arisen when surrogate mothers have either refused to relinquish the infant or have had a change of heart during the grace period which all states require prior to finalizing any adoption procedure. In cases in which the surrogate mother is awarded custody of the baby, she has the legal option of suing the prospective parents (as the male is the baby's biological father) for child support until the child comes of age.

Although surrogate mother cases have recently captured the media's limelight, single women using artificial insemination to have a child have sometimes found themselves involved in custody battles as well. That's what happened recently to two California women who decided to have a baby and raise the child together.

After jointly interviewing several men, they chose one to be the sperm donor. The artificial insemination process was successfully completed by a physician, and nine months later one of the women gave birth to a baby boy. The day after the baby was born, the man who had acted as the sperm donor visited the child at the hospital. After the baby went home, the man continued his visits and even set up a trust fund for the child.

When his presence became intrusive, the women requested that his visits stop. They had wanted a sperm donor, not a father for the baby, and they felt that those specifications had been made clear in their initial agreement. Now they were faced with a man whom they hardly knew, yet who seemed determined to become a significant person in the baby's life.

Once rebuffed by the women, the baby's sperm donor went to court to demand legal recognition as the baby's father as well as visitation rights. He eventually won both in two California courts of law. According to the trial judge, ". . . you are going to have a hard time convincing this court to call him (the man acting as the sperm donor) anything but the father of that child because I will not do that to that boy. . . . He wants to be a normal kid, like any other kid."[4]

Ironically, if the woman who had given birth had been married, the sperm donor could not have won the paternity case. In the majority of states, statutory law now considers the husband of an artificially inseminated woman to be the child's father. However, because of her marital status, the judge in this case in effect rendered her powerless to retain control of the situation.[5]

Other questions of legal responsibility involving surrogate mothers have yet to be determined. For example, carrying a fetus to term and delivering the child can involve serious risks to a woman's health. One surrogate mother, who had undergone a torturously painful sixteen-hour span in the labor and delivery room, finally gave birth to a healthy, beautiful baby boy. The infant spent the first moments of his life in the arms of his new prospective parents, who had been present at the surrogate's side throughout her difficult ordeal.

Immediately following the birth, the surrogate mother's medical condition took a serious turn for the worse. Looking back now on her experience, the woman claims that the fear on her doctor's face was evident. The surrogate mother had begun to hemorrhage.

She bled for over an hour. Her physician had described her condition to her husband as touch and go. She did, however, survive. If she had died, could her husband and the children surviving her have sued the prospective adoptive couple for damages? After all, they would have been deprived of the emotional and tangible services of a wife and mother.

What recourse does a surrogate mother, whose body has sustained serious injuries as a result of the birth, have? Can the couple with whom she contracted be made to pay for her follow-up medical care? Should there be a ceiling on the period of time for which they are liable? Can the prospective adoptive parents be considered in any way responsible if it is medically determined that as a result of complications occurring during this pregnancy, any future pregnancies might entail serious risks to the surrogate mother's well-being?

In this respect, the prospective parents would have inadvertently rendered her incapable of working any longer as a surrogate mother. Should a surrogate mother be regarded as an independent contractor or is she working for someone else? The full extent of the surrogate's rights and obligations, as well as those of the prospective parents, have yet to be determined.

Under contract law, when one party breaches or violates the terms of a contract, the other party is usually entitled to "damages." Securing damages entails getting a court order that will require the party who violated the contract's terms to pay a sum of money to the other party. However, prospective parents who are awarded monetary damages in court, because a surrogate mother with whom they had contracted decided to keep the baby, may not derive very much satisfaction from "winning" the case.

The vast majority of surrogate mothers come from low-income groups. Carrying and giving birth to a child is not an easy or painless task, but economic necessity has led many surrogate mothers to accept the risks involved. Most of these women have other children to raise and help support. Some even work at low-paying jobs while acting as a surrogate, in addition to caring for their own children. As a result, many of these women would be unable to pay if damages were awarded to the other party in court.

Under contract law, the second legal course of action available to an injured or wronged party when the other party breaches a contract involves a court's demand for a "specific performance." In such instances, the court orders the defaulting party to do that which was originally agreed to in the contract.

However, in surrogate mother situations it would be extremely difficult for a judge to either order a woman to carry a baby to term against her will *or* to surrender her own child if she wishes to keep the baby. In instances in which this might occur, it is unlikely that a decision of this nature would be upheld by a higher court.

A contract to give birth is unique. It is not the same

as ordering a builder to correct a construction flaw. A surrogate mother contract is unlike a contract for other services, because the fulfillment of the terms would actually entail the physical invasion of the contractor's body.

A surrogate mother carrying a fetus cannot simply walk off the job. The work contracted for is taking place inside of her. Most judges would be extremely reluctant to put a surrogate mother in jail to prevent her from having an abortion. Even in cases involving more typical contracts for personal services, judges tend to award damages rather than specific performance. In such instances, the judges have determined that requiring the party to fulfill the contract's terms against her will would be too close to slavery.

Is a surrogate mother contract then actually worthless? Under the present circumstances, it is generally agreed that the prospective parents contracting for the surrogate's services are not adequately protected. It's been argued that since surrogacy contracts exist in a hazy area of both public opinion and the law, those who choose to enter them must do so cautiously. Any contract that appears to be largely unenforceable must be entered into at one's own risk.

However, it may be that such reasoning is excessively hard on childless individuals. For some couples, using a surrogate may be the only way possible to have a child that is in some way genetically linked to them.

To erase some of the doubts and fears that currently accompany a surrogacy situation, the process may require legislation as well as strict regulation in order to ensure the rights and protection of everyone involved. As Professor W. Marshall Prettyman of Seton Hall University Law School in New Jersey told the *New York Times* on the issue, "As far as any security for people entering into a surrogate relationship, that's going to have to wait until after the Legislature does something."[6]

One suggested step would be to establish clear regulations governing the procedure and a state regulatory board to oversee and administer petitions for surrogate mothers in each state. Private surrogacy agreements would be made illegal for the protection of everyone involved, including that of the unborn baby. This action might help to prevent a future mass production of human beings for solely monetary purposes.

The board would act much as an adoption agency currently does. It would interview and screen prospective parents to ensure that they were capable of adequately raising a child. This would prevent individuals already turned down by an adoption agency from gaining possession of a child despite the fact that this might not be in the baby's best interests. At the very least, the board would have an opportunity to prevent individuals with a history of child molestation and exploitation from purchasing a baby.

The board would screen potential surrogate mothers also. They might attempt to recruit women whose main motive would be to help others. They also would try to ensure that the women selected would be best able psychologically to give the baby to its new parents. However, this would not mean that any state board would be empowered to force a woman to give up her baby if she's certain that she is unable to do so. But prior screening by a team of unbiased professionals might best eliminate the women most likely to experience problems in this area.

To further prevent exploitation, all fees involved would be firmly set and paid through the state agency. Technically, it is currently illegal to buy or sell a baby. So far surrogate mother arrangements have managed to circumvent these laws, by claiming that the fees exchanged are paid for the "services" which the surrogate mother performs. They argue that the actual babies are never paid for. This would help to end any threats or extortion attempts made by surrogate mothers during their pregnancies to prospective parents. It would also help to ensure that the surrogate mothers receive the full amount of money they were originally promised.

Perhaps most importantly, a nonprofit state agency would eliminate the need for the new commercial agencies that have sprung up in recent years to match surrogate mothers with prospective parents. These are unregulated profit-making agencies that offer their services for a fee. Today, anyone can open a surrogate mother agency. Doctors, lawyers, businessmen, and housewives, among others, have started these enterprises to meet the ever-growing demand for babies.

As William Handel, a Los Angeles attorney who helps run a separate nonprofit surrogate mother information center, told *People*: "You could rent an office, hang up a shingle that says 'Surrogate Mothers Inc., BABIES FOR YOU, CHEAP,' and no one could stop you."[7]

Frustrated and desperate couples often find their way into these offices. By this time, they have usually exhausted all other opportunities to secure a child. Some couples may be willing to use their life savings for the chance to start a family. Functioning under the prolonged pressure of excessive strain, guilt, and unrealized hopes, these individuals may have acquired unrealistic expectations of what a baby will do for their lives as well as for their marriages.

The typical total fee charged by these agencies is generally about $25,000. The cost includes the surrogate mother's fee plus any legal, medical, or counseling costs involved. The prospective parents' expenses can skyrocket once they begin to pay for the surrogate's living and travel expenses, if her home is far from the agency, and again if repeated attempts at artificial insemination are necessary. It is unlikely that any surrogate-seeking couple who can afford to pay the fees will be turned away by a commercial surrogate center.

In addition, it would also be unprofitable for a

commercial organization to turn away surrogate mother candidates because of stringent screening procedures. A surrogate agency that rejected too many potential applicants would be cutting down on its own profits.

Several such agencies only ask the women wishing to become surrogate mothers to undergo a short interview. Some surrogate mothers have even claimed that the agencies with which they dealt never asked them whether they had been under psychiatric care, had taken medication for anxiety or depression, or felt that they might experience difficulty in surrendering the child.

Sometimes prospective parents or customers are not well-screened either. In some cases, they need only submit a recommendation from their physician for the procedure along with a superficial health report. At times, agencies may even waive these minor requirements.

In defense of their scant screening procedures, some commercial agencies have argued that every individual has the intrinsic right to procreate, and that no human being or agency should have the authority to determine that someone either can or cannot have a child.

Others who wish to see surrogate motherhood regulated by a state organization argue that commercial agencies do not consider the newborn baby's rights, despite the fact that their decisions may greatly influence the child's future. It is highly doubtful that a nonprofit agency would be tempted to use unsuitable surrogate mothers to ease the shortage, as such actions would only discredit the agency's reputation. Therefore, once the personal profit motive is removed, the screening process would probably be completed more objectively and professionally.

As one Kentucky circuit judge said of the profit-making agencies, "Children need the protection of someone other than those motivated by personal gain.

We don't know what kind of environment they're going to. I don't think you can sell them like apples and oranges."[8]

It may be justifiably argued that it would be impossible to ever actually ban or even totally control surrogate mother situations. Private arrangements of this nature have been secretly made in the past and will undoubtedly occur in the future. The artificial insemination of a woman may not always require a physician's assistance. Some individuals have successfully completed the process using only medical books and paraphernalia purchased from a drug store. When that has failed, some prospective fathers have even engaged in sexual intercourse with the selected surrogate mother in order to have the woman conceive a child for his wife and himself. Those who are against firm regulations for surrogate mothers believe that such measures would not prohibit surrogate mother agreements, but rather would only serve to drive the process underground.

Most proponents of state-regulated surrogate mother pacts agree that firm legal guidelines may not curtail illegal surrogate activities; however, they may reduce the many recurring problems involved. In addition, if state-approved surrogate mother agreements were available, fewer people would seek out the private solutions that might involve unscrupulous individuals.

So far, the unusual dilemmas posed by the new technology of fertility and conception have sought their solutions in American courts of law. However, lacking proper legal guidelines, the various judicial rulings on these matters have been varied and diverse. Most cases go on to be appealed in still higher courts. Some in the justice system have argued that surrogate mother arrangements should not be determined in courts, but are instead "matters of legislative concern."

Although legal guidelines may be sorely needed to iron out the difficulties, political caution about what voters really want and concerns regarding the illegal invasion of privacy may continue to inhibit immediate governmental reform. More than a dozen states have witnessed the death or delay of legislation to control the process.

There is also a wide range of viewpoints regarding the type of legislation needed. Some elected officials, such as Richard Fitzpatrick, a Democrat in the Michigan state legislature, have advocated that the prospective parents who plan to rear the child be granted "all paternal rights and responsibilities for a child regardless of the condition of the child, conceived through a fertility technique."[9] Other legislators have drafted laws to ban surrogate mother arrangements altogether, making such agreements punishable by both fines and imprisonment.

Perhaps the mixed feelings generated by the new birth technologies was best expressed by Senator Albert Gore, a Tennessean with four children of his own, who said, "There is something unnatural, even violent, about a procedure that takes a newborn from its mother's arms and gives it to another by virtue of a contract. But I don't think I'm in favor of outlawing it. The touching search for children may justify a great many things that make others of us who are more fortunate uncomfortable."[10]

4
Portrait of a Surrogate

Turning away from the baby was the hardest thing I've ever done in my life. I didn't look back. I knew that if I did, I might not be able to handle it. It was the saddest good-bye I've ever known, even though I had told myself again and again during the pregnancy that it was really not my baby. The tears refused to stop. I cried for three days after I got home.[1]

A surrogate mother is a special kind of mother. She is a woman who conceives, carries, and gives birth to a baby, only to give her child away to someone else. Do these women consider themselves mothers or human manufacturers of a product designed to bring fulfillment and joy to infertile women and their husbands? They've been scorned by some, while admired by others. But whatever the viewpoint, one haunting question still remains: Can a woman who conceives and gives birth to a baby ever *not* be considered that child's mother?

Surrogate motherhood is certainly not a new phenomenon. In fact, there is a good deal of evidence to suggest that the practice went on during Biblical times. When Sarah was unable to give her husband Abraham a child, she sent him to lie with her handmaiden Hagar. Her intent was for Abraham to impregnate Hagar so that Sarah could have a child through her servant.

Perhaps the best-known study of surrogate mothers was conducted in 1983 by Michigan psychiatrist Philip J. Parker.[2] Parker isolated the three main reasons why women volunteer to be surrogate mothers as follows: 1) the desire for financial support; 2) the desire to be pregnant; and 3) the desire to work out or reconcile a past trauma in their lives that in some way related to the experience of giving birth; for example, having had an abortion or given up a child for adoption.

Dr. Parker described the typical surrogate mother as being a high-school-educated Christian woman who is approximately twenty-five years of age.

The actual experiences of surrogate mothers may differ vastly, regardless of their reasons for becoming one. Some have described their experience as being rewarding and fulfilling. Carolyn Williams, a young surrogate mother in her twenties, was delighted to learn that the physician's attempts had finally succeeded and that she was already pregnant. She wanted to share her joy with the prospective mother, a businesswoman in her forties named Barbara. So Ms. Williams sent Barbara a large bouquet of helium-filled balloons, along with a rhyming note which read: "Roses are Red/Violets are Blue/ We're going to have a baby/Congratulations to you too."

Carolyn and Barbara went to the obstetrician together, because Carolyn hoped to make the prospective mother feel as though she were actually having the baby herself. Carolyn Williams gave birth to a healthy baby boy, whom she turned over to the adoptive parents.

As she told *Newsweek*, "I just wanted to do it for the

whole world. I felt God gave me this gift. This has been a calling for me. . . . I left the hospital with a picture in my mind of happiness, a happy family."³

Becky McKnight, of Los Angeles, California, was already a mother of three when she decided to become a surrogate mother. Several years ago, Ms. McKnight began to think seriously about the idea for the first time after working in the office of three obstetricians whose practice dealt largely with infertility.

Seeing the anguish and disappointment on the faces of the many couples who were unable to have their own families, Ms. McKnight saw the prospect of acting as a surrogate as a chance to provide a worthwhile alternative. Becky McKnight became a surrogate mother and had a baby by Caesarean section.

Elizabeth X, mother of two, acted as a surrogate mother when she gave birth to a baby boy on March 24, 1983, for a Colorado couple. She described her reasons as follows:

> *When I first heard about surrogate motherhood in March of 1981, I thought what a wonderful alternative it was for couples who can't have children. I kept thinking about it, turning it over in my mind.*
>
> *I had had an abortion several years ago which still troubled me. It was traumatic, and I couldn't get it out of my mind. I had wanted another child, but it was impossible for us economically to raise another one. I couldn't replace the aborted child, but I wanted to compensate for it in some way.*⁴

Despite the objections of some of her family members and friends, Elizabeth X went ahead with her plan to become a surrogate mother. Although she experienced some difficulty in the delivery room and later in separating from the baby, she was eventually able to resolve her feelings.

> *Only then was I able to stop crying, and I haven't wept since. Until that moment, I had felt an emptiness without the baby in my arms. I had become confident, of course, that the child would be well loved and cared for—he is the most precious thing in their lives—but I couldn't breathe easy until I knew [adoptive mother] Susan's full maternal bonding was there.*[5]

Deborah Snyder, who believes that motherhood is the essence of life, claims that she wanted to become a surrogate mother in order to do something significant and meaningful for others. According to Ms. Snyder:

> *I understand that some women love being pregnant. Not me. That wasn't it at all. When you tell people that you're going to be a surrogate mother, some think, "She's trying to be a saint." Well, it's really true. The last few years I'd been thinking that I really hadn't done anything for anyone except myself and my family. I thought this would be important.*[6]

At times, female family members have acted as surrogate mothers for their infertile sisters or cousins. Sherry King of Fort Lauderdale, Florida, already had a young daughter named Sarah when she agreed to become a surrogate mother for her sister. Sherry's older sister Carole had had a hysterectomy at the age of twenty-one. This made it impossible for her to ever have a biological child of her own.

Ironically, Sherry King and her husband had planned to have another child of their own at just about the same time that Sherry's sister approached her about being a surrogate. In order to give her sister a child, Sherry's own family's agenda would have to be delayed until the task was completed.

In addition, Mrs. King and her husband had to abstain from marital relations themselves until they were certain that Sherry had conceived through artificial insemination. Mrs. King's brother-in-law was to be the sperm donor. It was essential to everyone that the baby's biological father be Sherry's brother-in-law, Ernie.

The sisters and their husbands called the endeavor their family project. Finally, in December 1983, after several months of trying, Sherry King found that she had become pregnant. Christmas had come early for all of them.

Everything went well until about sixteen weeks later. In March 1984 Sherry suffered a miscarriage. It was as if there had been a death in the family; everyone grieved for the lost child. The prospective adoptive mother became extremely depressed over the loss, but her sister Sherry assured her that they would try again.

And that's exactly what they did. Sherry once again conceived through artificial insemination, and eventually gave birth to a healthy baby girl. Carole had acted as her sister's coach during Sherry's labor. The two women maintained eye contact throughout the birth, and with each painful contraction, Sherry reached out to grasp her sister's shoulder. Carole spoke gently to Sherry, trying to ease her discomfort.

Carole remained present, along with both the women's husbands, in the delivery room. As Sherry pushed to ease the baby's head through the birth canal, Carole whispered, "I'm so scared! This is it!" Afterwards, she confided to her sister that all the while she had been silently praying for a healthy, normal baby.

Unfortunately, the baby's delivery proved to be extremely painful. But when it was all over, Sherry recalled that she felt as though the end result had been worth what she had gone through. At last Carole and her husband were the proud parents of a baby girl, whom they named Kristen Jennifer.

Today, whenever Sherry is asked how she was able to give up her own baby, she states that she never felt

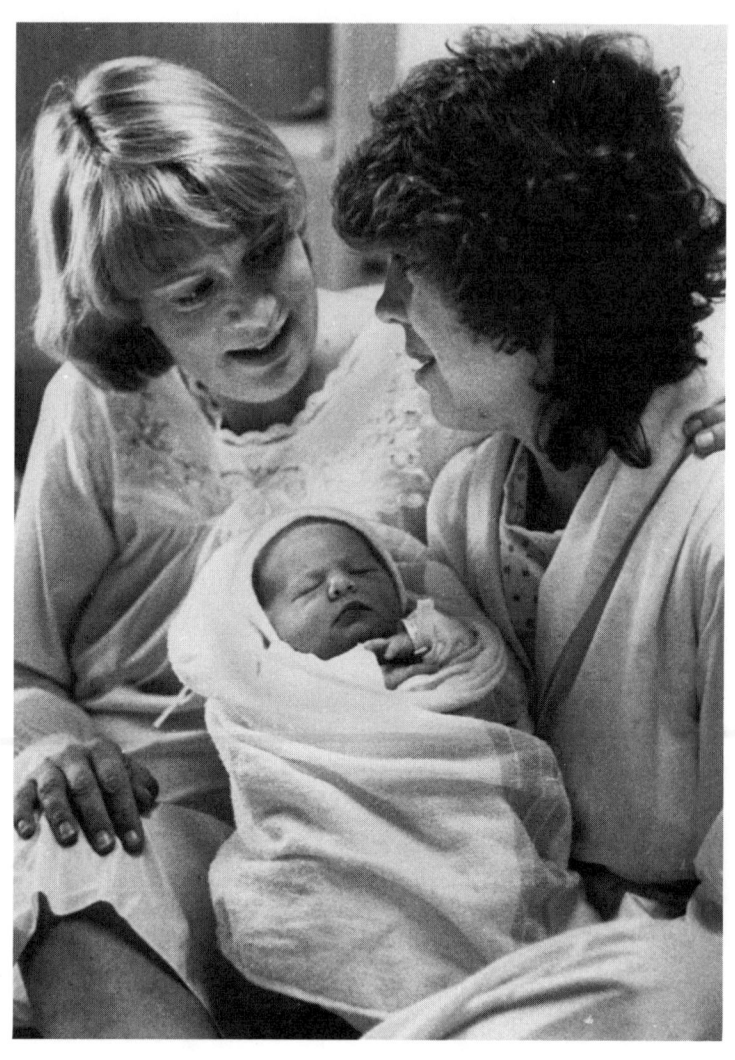

Sherry King (left) gave birth to Kristen Jennifer for her sister, Carole Jalbert. Mrs. King was artificially inseminated with sperm from Mrs. Jalbert's husband.

as though Kristen Jennifer was actually hers. Instead, Sherry King viewed being a surrogate as lending her body to her sister. For her, carrying Kristen to term was more like babysitting her sister's daughter for nine months than actually becoming the baby's mother.

As Sherry expressed to her sister at a Christmas family gathering: "I can't believe it myself, but I don't have any motherly feelings toward Kristen. I love her like a niece—the same way you feel about Sarah [Sherry and her husband's daughter]."[7]

Karen Mills, a married mother of two, also chose to act as a surrogate mother for her sister, Kit. After learning that her Fallopian tubes were blocked and badly scarred due to a severe infection, Kit had been told that she would never be able to bear children. Kit and her husband, Mark, had explored the options of adoption as well as in vitro fertilization, but they had become discouraged at the prospect of long waiting lists and an expensive attempt at a fertilization process with an extremely low success rate.

After several tries at artificial insemination using Kit's husband Mark's sperm, Karen Mills conceived on December 10, 1982. Unfortunately, it wasn't long before Karen realized that the pregnancy might be difficult. As she described it in an article appearing in *Ladies Home Journal*: "And it was soon evident that this pregnancy wasn't going to be quite so easy. The life growing within me seemed to derive a great deal of pleasure from giving me morning sickness all day long, and later from kicking me in the ribs and being generally unpleasant to its aunt-to-be."[8]

However, when the baby finally arrived, Karen's labor only lasted three and a half hours. Kit had remained at her sister's side throughout the delivery, rubbing her back and offering words of encouragement. Karen Mills gave birth to a healthy baby girl, whom Kit and her husband named Jessica.

Watching her sister and brother-in-law with their new baby made Karen feel certain that she had done the right thing. She wrote the following about her experience as a surrogate mother:

> *When I saw Kit and Mark holding Jessica in their arms, I knew for sure that the morning sickness had been worthwhile. I had never seen two such happy people in my life. I also recognized my own sadness that my role in the process was finished. I would never again be needed by my sister in such a special way.*
>
> *Yet I had no desire to hold on to the child that was now hers, and most important, I was grateful that I would be able to pay her back, in a way, for all the love and support she had always shown me.*[9]

When Jessica is old enough to understand, her parents intend to share the story of her birth with her. Although Karen describes herself as the carrier, she knows that Jessica would have never been born if it weren't for her sister Kit. Karen Mills hopes that one day Jessica will understand how much two sisters can mean to one another, and how much Kit loves the daughter she so desperately wanted.

Although Sherry King's and Karen Mills' stories had happy endings, this isn't always the case. At times, women who, before they became pregnant, claimed that they'd have no problem relinquishing the baby, have later found it painful to do so.

The atmosphere and regulations set up by the various surrogacy centers can also have a bearing on the reactions of both the surrogate mothers and the prospective parents. Different agencies handle what may prove to be a strained and delicate relationship between the contracted parties in various ways. While some agencies encourage the couples and the surrogate mothers to get to know one another and spend some time together, other centers have strict rules against this.

Elizabeth Kane (pseudonym), one of the first women to sign a contract to become a surrogate mother. She signed away all parental rights to the child and has since had second thoughts about surrogate mother contracts.

For example, one surrogate mother agency in Chevy Chase, Maryland, provides clients with physical descriptions and medical histories of the surrogates, but will not release the names of the parties involved. Although anonymity may reduce the risk of possible problems in the future, a surrogate mother forced to give up her baby to a home which she knows little about, and which has not been subjected to the thorough screening conducted by legitimate adoption agencies, may suffer serious pangs of conscience.

Elizabeth Kane (pseudonym), a mother of three from Illinois, was among the first women to sign a contract to become a surrogate mother. Although initially she had been in favor of the procedure, she has since had second thoughts. Ms. Kane told *Time* magazine: "I would still give the birth mother first choice. If she does give up the child, psychological counseling should be provided for her after delivery."[10] Ms. Kane went on to stress that throughout the surrogate mother's pregnancy, the contracting couples are always thoughtful and solicitous to the woman. However, their attitude usually changes abruptly following the birth. According to Kane, "Once you've delivered, they are not interested in you. We give up so much to have a child for another woman, and then we don't have any rights."[11]

Ms. Kane has also raised the question as to whether using surrogate mothers is in any way fair to women. As she told *Newsweek*, "All you're doing is transferring the pain from one woman to another, from a woman who is in pain from her infertility to a woman who has to give up her baby."[12]

According to an article in the *New York Times*, interviews with half a dozen surrogate mothers revealed that a widely publicized custody-fight, waged by a New Jersey surrogate mother, had reawakened both joyful and sorrowful feelings in them about their experience. One surrogate had this to say about the case:

> *Until Mary Beth's case came to light, none of us knew who we were and none of us was willing to talk about it, because giving up a baby is not something we're proud of. . . . I have lost a baby and I don't say that out of pity for myself, but for the hundreds and maybe thousands of other surrogates who will reach that point of understanding some day, just as I did. Then they will look in the mirror and say, "My God, what have I done?"*[13]

Another surrogate mother from northern California who was interviewed expressed similar feelings and doubts. "I started having doubts as soon as I was pregnant. They had these girls on TV saying how easy it was and how good it made them feel, but nobody warned me how strange it is to have a baby and not keep it."[14]

Maria Dotterer, a machinist's wife from near Treasure City, Michigan, had agreed to act as a surrogate mother for a Connecticut couple. But after giving birth to a baby girl in March 1986, she found that separating from her child was excruciatingly painful despite the fact that she had tried to look at her contract as a business agreement. According to Mrs. Dotterer,

> *When they came by from the hospital to say goodbye, I told myself that I wasn't going to cry, but I did. I told myself all along it would be easy, but it wasn't. ... It was hard for me to take the money. I rationalized that we'd use it to get something for the kids and pay some bills and get a used car we needed, because if the money was just for me I'd feel as if I'd sold her, and it would be dirty money.*[15]

Although some women who become surrogate mothers do so fully aware of the consequences that may accompany their actions, others claim that they were not given full information about the procedures involved. This occurred recently in San Diego, California, when a surrogate mother sued a couple for child support and custody of an eight-month-old child, whom she said she was tricked into carrying.

According to the surrogate mother, twenty-year-old Alejandra Munoz, she agreed to come from Mexico to the United States in September 1985 to conceive a child for her second cousin, Nettie Haro. Ms. Haro, who was thirty-seven years old at the time, had an eighteen-year-old daughter from a previous marriage, and she had been warned by her doctor that trying to have another child might damage her health.

Nettie Haro and her husband, Mario, testified in court that Alejandra Munoz originally agreed to bear the child as an act of kindness, but later demanded money and threatened to have an abortion. The Haros claimed that Munoz tried to blackmail them two months after she conceived, demanding $5,000.

Ms. Munoz, on the other hand, has sworn that she was deceived by her cousins, saying that they told her that she would have to carry the fetus only until a transplant of the fetus could be performed from her to Ms. Haro. Once she learned that there'd be no transplant, Ms. Munoz felt that the baby she was carrying was her own, and she refused to give the child up. On June 25, 1986, she gave birth to a baby girl, Lydia Michelle. Almost immediately, the child became the object of a fierce court custody battle.

After a good deal of testimony was heard from both sides, the attorneys representing Munoz and the Haros reached a settlement that was acceptable to both sides. The agreement, read by Superior Court Judge William Pate, specified that the baby Lydia Michelle would presently live with the Haro family. However, Ms. Munoz was granted overnight visitation rights, and as Lydia Michelle matured, she would spend more time at the home of her biological mother.

The joint custody agreement ordered both sides not to make any disparaging remarks about the other in the child's presence. It also forbade Ms. Munoz, a Mexican citizen, from leaving the country with her baby.

Although most prospective parents generally do not wish the child to be involved with its surrogate mother, in some cases surrogate mothers have arranged for occasional visitation rights as part of the original contractual agreement. That's the way Peggy Pressler, a surrogate mother and mother of two from Canton, Ohio, had wanted it.

Surrogate mother Alejandra Munoz holds her baby. She had agreed to carry the fetus for one month for a couple, until a transplant could be performed. However, she had to carry the baby to full term and subsequently sought custody of the child.

In 1985 she bore a son for a California couple. As Ms. Pressler told the press, "Sally and Everett [adoptive parents] agreed from the beginning that we should be able to see the baby later. If they had said no contact, I would have said no, because that's very important to me and I wouldn't have done it."[16]

Ms. Pressler, who had been an adopted child herself, continued, "I thought it would be very important later on for this child to understand what happened and to know who I was. I was pretty much in the dark when I was growing up and it only made everything more confusing to me."[17]

Some surrogate mothers, who in retrospect deeply regret what they've done, reject the term "surrogate mother." They stress that women who voluntarily place their unwanted children up for adoption are usually referred to as "birth mothers." These women feel that the label surrogate is used to somehow lessen the full impact of having a child and giving it away to others for a predetermined sum of money.

They argue that being called a surrogate can never make you any less of the baby's mother, but may only help to enhance a woman's misunderstanding of what she's actually done. Pointing out that after a time both the defenses and the money run out, they warn that women who become surrogate mothers may eventually have to deal with the most painful reality of their lives.

5
Moral and Ethical Issues

The new reproductive technologies, including surrogate motherhood, pose an array of intriguing and sometimes disturbing moral and ethical issues. In fact, at the University of Michigan's Ninth Conference on Ethics, Humanism, and Medicine, Professor Samuel Gorovitz referred to the issue of surrogate mothers as another example of how rapidly advanced technology "has outstripped our social wisdom" and capacity to deal with potential consequences.

How shall we weigh the liabilities and benefits of surrogate motherhood to society, to our notions of family, to the couple, and to the surrogate mother? Among the ethical concerns raised is: How shall we determine whether surrogacy does a disservice to the child who is created?

SOCIETAL ISSUES

Critics of surrogate mothers and other reproductive technologies have stressed that it isn't always necessary to be biologically related to one's offspring in order to experience being a parent. They point to the fact that although there are many homeless children in America today, these youths often grow up without parents because they aren't considered suitable for adoption.

What makes a child a desirable candidate for adoption? Unfortunately, adoption agencies cite that the children most sought after are healthy, white infants. Despite the fact that an older child, a minority group child, or a young person with physical or emotional disabilities may desperately need the love and support provided by a stable and concerned family, these are the very children who may pass their early years in a series of foster homes and institutions.

When the problem is viewed on a broader global level, the use of surrogate mothers and other "high tech" means of conception appears even more nonsensical to some. They ask why anyone would find it necessary to go to such lengths to create more babies, when high birth rates and burgeoning populations represent one of the world's most challenging problems.

Beyond that argument—of further populating an already overpopulated world—lies an even more controversial issue. Some have charged that the new reproductive technologies, including surrogate motherhood, serve to perpetuate racism and advance the concept of eugenics—the idea that the species can be improved through selective breeding. Perhaps among the best examples of this may be the Repository for Germinal Choice located in Escondido, California.

This institute, which opened its doors in 1980 and performs artificial insemination by donor, had boasted that it would impregnate women using sperm donated by Nobel prize winners. Although only three Nobel prize winners cooperated in the endeavor, the institute's founder, Robert Graham, remained enthusiastic about his promised product. As he described the repository's

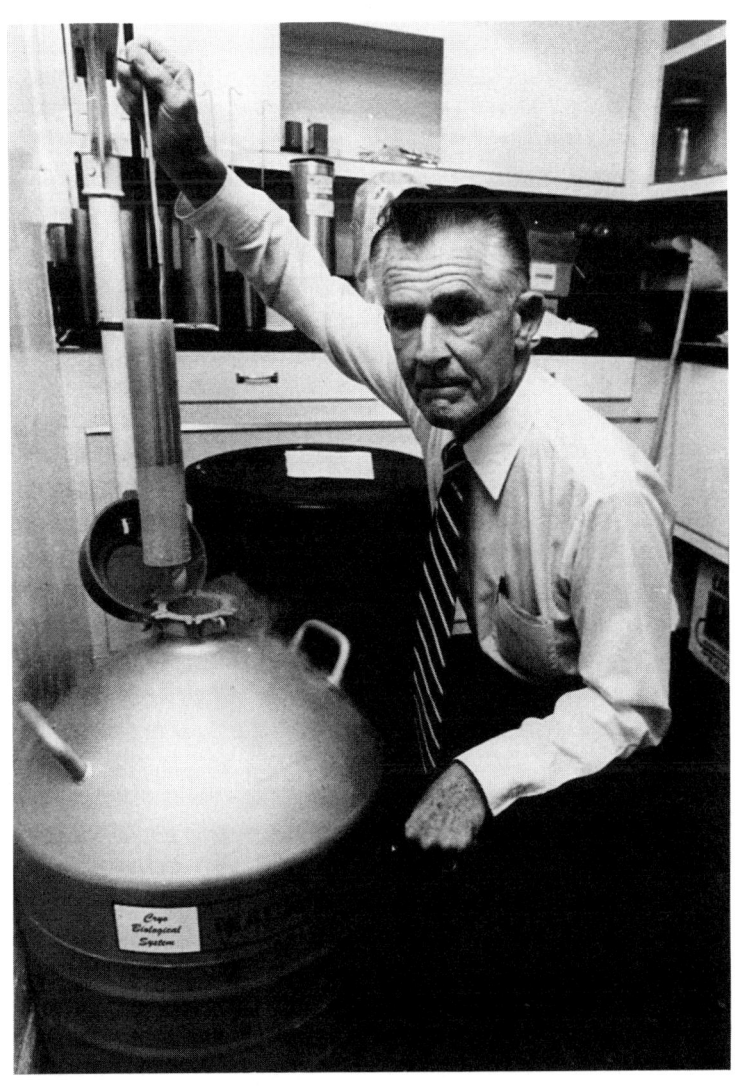

*Robert Graham displays a
container holding the sperm
of one of his donors at his
underground laboratory
in California.*

children in an interview in *Time* magazine, "We're proud of our results. . . . These kids will sail through school. We are indicating how good human beings can have it."[1]

Although most parents would prefer a bright child as an ideal, intellectual ability may not be the only variable considered in what could turn into a selective breeding process. Today, many commercial sperm banks offer prospective parents full information on the physical characteristics of the donors. In addition, couples seeking a surrogate mother for their child are often especially concerned with the woman's physical attractiveness.

Although the apparent concern with appearance is most often justified on the grounds that it is helpful for a child to resemble its prospective parents, some people fear that before long potential parents will be attempting to produce only blonds instead of brunettes, tall rather than short children, or perhaps boys instead of girls. One couple—both the husband and wife were short and had dark brown hair—insisted that the surrogate mother agency with which they worked locate a tall, blond, glamorous surrogate mother for them, regardless of the cost.

In Essen, Germany, a fertility clinic advertises for sperm donors for artificial insemination and specifies: "no fat men, no long ears, no hook noses. . . ." As New York Theological Seminary's professor of ethics, the Rev. Roger Shinn, told *Time* magazine, "We can talk in impressive pseudoscientific terms about what we want to help society, but as long as genetic manipulation is the motive, what we would be doing is what Hitler intended to do."[2]

There are numerous other objections to the use of surrogate mothers. Some people feel that the process dehumanizes childbirth, which they believe should result from a deep sense of love and commitment between a man and a woman. What are the social consequences of manipulating a basic human act through the wonders of advanced technology? Will scientifically created parenthood and surrogate mothers serve to make childbearing so distant and impersonal that one will simply order a baby as if it were a customized car or mail order goods? While the arrival of a desperately wanted child may seem the welcome answer to a personal prayer, technological parenthood may have too many of the trappings of a business. The birth of a baby is the creation of a human being, and any situation that renders it otherwisay seem unsettling or even frightening to some.

In an article in the *New York Times Magazine*, the boyfriend of a surrogate mother described his feelings about her actions as follows: "Just look at her, would you look at her. Her stomach was that flat the day she left the hospital and she doesn't have a stretch mark on her. I'll take care of her when she's pregnant again, but the baby means absolutely nothing. It's like watching someone's car for nine months. We're in it for the money; it's a business. That's the way we look at it."[3]

In response to the increased interest in surrogate mothers, in May 1983 the American College of Obstetricians and Gynecologists (ACOG) issued a set of guidelines for doctors entitled "Ethical Issues in Surrogate Motherhood." According to the two-page document, the ACOG "has significant reservations about this approach to parenthood."

The document warns physicians against becoming involved in recruiting surrogates for their patients or investing in commercial surrogate mother agencies. The guidelines also point out that baby selling is both morally and legally reprehensible, and that it can be extremely difficult to distinguish between "payments made for the service of carrying a child and for the child itself."

The ACOG guidelines leave the final decision as to

whether or not to take part in surrogate agreements up to the individual physician. However, it stresses that doctors should carefully consider the ethical, legal, psychological, and societal implications involved, in addition to medical factors.

Would the general acceptance of surrogate mothers, bound by contract to commercially produce babies for others, mean that our society was ready to accept a dual definition of motherhood? Would it now become commonplace for a child to have two mothers? One would be the biological mother, who is genetically related to the baby but parts with the child at birth for a predetermined sum. The child's other mother would be the baby's psychological or care-giving mother, who is not biologically related to the baby but is instead married to the infant's father.

As Dr. Arthur Caplan, a philosopher at the Hastings Center—a research institute on biomedical ethics in Briarcliff Manor, New York—told the *New York Times*, "This case shakes the certainty of defining the term 'mother.' It's socially and culturally disturbing. It takes away a reference point. It chips away at our certainty of understanding our concept of 'mother'. Is it the environmental and social shaper or the person who provides the hereditary blueprint?"[4]

ISSUES AFFECTING THE COUPLES AND INDIVIDUALS WHO USE SURROGATES

If surrogate mothers are to become a staple of American life, under what conditions should they exist? Should anyone with adequate funds be permitted to order a baby at whim?

Individuals have turned to surrogate mothers for a variety of reasons. In some instances, surrogacy may be seen as an alternative to a medical problem involving the woman's reproductive system or a serious health problem that would make pregnancy inadvisable or even dangerous. Although many people are sympathetic to infertile couples who desperately want a baby, should the use of surrogate mothers be permitted for nonmedical reasons as well?

What about career women who may wish to have a child, but feel that a pregnancy might drain their time and energy as well as disrupt their careers? If they can afford it, should they be permitted to pay another woman to have a baby for them?

Some women may also wish to avoid pregnancy because of the unsightly effect it may have on their slim figures as well as on their overall appearance. A pregnancy could certainly at least temporarily defer the earning potential of an actress or model. At times, some women have expressed their concern over the importance of remaining physically attractive to their spouses or boyfriends. Still other women who wish to have a child may be only too glad to pay someone else to experience morning sickness, the discomfort of feeling bloated, and the pain of childbirth.

The reasons for turning to a surrogate mother may range from that of serious medical causes to seeking a convenient way to start a family. But if the law is to eventually intervene in surrogate agreements, who should be legally entitled to use a surrogate's services and for what reasons? Some proponents of surrogacy feel that such contracts should be made available only to married couples in which the wife has been medically certified as being unable to reproduce.

Under current conditions, there is another inherent factor limiting access to the use of surrogate mothers: the financial status of the potential adoptive parents or parent. With costs sometimes amounting to over thirty thousand dollars, the process has thus far remained largely in the exclusive domain of the affluent. In instances in which the woman who wishes to become pregnant is infertile, should health insurance cover the costs involved in surrogate arrangements in much the same way it would pay for the costs incurred during a pregnancy and delivery or an abortion?

Some lawyers have argued that the Constitution ensures the right of all Americans to reproduce. Therefore, they reason that anyone who wants a child should be able to avail themselves of the service. Under these circumstances, it may be difficult to establish guidelines that are not prejudicial.

In addition, many people firmly believe that in a free society, anyone should be able to do as he or she pleases, as long as no one is harmed. They feel that restrictions should not be placed on a surrogate mother's right to earn her living as she chooses, nor should limitations hamper the rights of childless individuals who can afford to pay for a surrogate mother's services.

ISSUES AFFECTING THE SURROGATE MOTHER AND HER FAMILY

Are surrogate mothers exploited by the very process into which they voluntarily enter? One vital concern raised by the existence of surrogate mother contracts is that of informed consent. Can surrogates ever be genuinely informed in advance about how they will feel after they carry the baby to term?

It may also be important to consider the effect of surrogate motherhood on the surrogate mother's other children, if she has them. Will these children be able to stand by and watch a child borne by their mother being given away or sold without having the transaction affect them?

Still another aspect to consider is this: if the services of surrogate mothers remain only affordable to the monied class, might these contracts help create a sort of lower class of woman breeders? Women who are extremely poor and undereducated might feel forced to produce and sell their babies to more prosperous women for a relatively modest fee. Some opponents of surrogate motherhood have expressed fears that women struggling for survival in poorer Third World nations might prove to be especially vulnerable targets for this type of exploitation.

To quote Dr. Doris Jonas Freed, co-chairperson of the surrogate-parenting committee of the New York State Bar Association, "We don't want breeders for people in a different financial strata. The money has to be played down."[5] Although Dr. Freed expressed her belief that surrogate agreements would probably eventually be nationally legalized, she added that it is also essential that strict procedures for psychological, physical, and genetic screening be enacted. According to Dr. Freed, "We want to end the pain wherever it's possible, for everyone."[6]

ISSUES AFFECTING THE UNBORN BABY

The long-term effects of being born out of a surrogate mother contract are still largely unknown. Unfortunately, the current, unregulated, commercial use of surrogate mothers may lead to practices that are not always in the child's best interests.

Might some childless couples so desperately desire a child that they'd be willing to accept an unsuitable person as their surrogate? Likewise, might surrogate mother arrangements allow some potentially unfit parents with ample funds to gain control over the life of an innocent child? Does society have the right, if not the obligation, to prevent children from being born under undesirable circumstances? For many, it is difficult to draw a definitive line indicating where the rights of the contracting individuals end and those of their human product—a new person—begin.

Other unsettled issues come into play following the

child's birth. For example, do the children of surrogate mothers have a right to know their genetic origins? If they wish to have contact with their biological mother while growing up, do they have that right? What are their inheritance rights with regard to their natural mothers?

RELIGIOUS ISSUES

Some individuals are against the use of surrogate mothers because they feel that it defies God's will. They believe that perhaps some women simply weren't meant to have children. However, proponents of surrogate agreements simply reply: God did not give us wings to fly, but we still have airplanes. They argue that God provided people with good minds to improve their lives; for many individuals, surrogate parenting is one way to achieve that. Claiming that it is hypocritical for the church to object to surrogate mothers as unnatural, some in favor of the procedure have pointed to the virgin birth, suggesting that Mary may have been the first surrogate mother.

Nevertheless, on March 10, 1987, the Vatican in Rome issued a new document entitled "Instruction on Respect for Human Life in Its Origins and on the Dignity of Procreation: Replies to Certain Questions of the Day," which called for *all* governments to put strict limitations on medical interference in human procreation. In a major doctrinal statement, the Roman Catholic Church called for laws prohibiting such practices as surrogate mothers, artificial insemination, embryo transfer, and experimentation on living embryos, among others.

The document warned, "The new technological possibilities which have opened up in the field of biomedicine require the intervention of political authorities and the legislator, since an uncontrolled application of such techniques could lead to unforeseeable and damaging consequences for civil society."

When interviewed, chief Vatican spokesperson Joaquin Navarro-Valls stressed that the recently released church document addressed a much broader audience than usual, in that "it asks government leaders, be they Catholic or not, to firmly impose moral norms on certain medical and scientific activities."[7]

The document states:

Thanks to the progress of biological and medical sciences, man has at his disposal ever more effective therapeutic resources; but he can also acquire new powers with unforeseeable consequences over human life at its very beginning and in its first stages. Various procedures now make it possible to intervene not only to assist but also to dominate the process of procreation. These techniques can enable man to take in hand his own destiny, but they also expose him to the temptation to go beyond the limits of a reasonable dominion over nature. They might constitute progress in the service of man, but they also involve serious risks. Many people are therefore expressing an urgent appeal that in interventions on procreation, the values and rights of the human person be safeguarded.

With specific regard to artificial insemination and surrogate mothers, the church document stated,

"Respect for the unity of marriage and for conjugal fidelity demands that the child be conceived in marriage; the bond existing between the husband and wife, accords the spouses in an objective and inalienable manner, the exclusive right to become father and mother solely through each other. Recourse to ... a third person ... constitutes a violation of the reciprocal commitment of the spouses and a grave lack in regard to that essential property of marriage which is its unity. ... it

> brings about and manifests a rupture between genetic parenthood, gestational parenthood and responsibility for upbringing. Such damage to the personal relationships within the family has repercussions on civil society. What threatens the unity and stability of the family is a source of dissension, disorder, and injustice in the whole of social life.
>
> ... Surrogate mothers represent an objective failure to meet the obligations of maternal love, of conjugal fidelity, and of responsible motherhood. It offends the dignity and the right of the child to be conceived, carried in the womb, brought into the world and brought up by his own parents, it sets up to the detriment of families, a division between the physical, psychological, and moral elements which constitute those families.

The Vatican document caused some dissent within the Catholic theological community. While some theologians and representatives of the church hierarchy in the United States have voiced their support for the Vatican's position, other Roman Catholic theologians have disagreed with parts of the document, especially the segments that oppose the use of artificial means to fertilize a woman's egg with her husband's sperm. As Rev. Richard A. McCormick, one of the nation's leading Catholic authorities on biomedical ethics, said in the *New York Times*: "I do not think the Vatican document is persuasive. The document argues that a child can be born only from a sexual act. The most that can be argued is that a child should be born within a marriage from a loving act. Sexual intercourse is not the only loving act."[8]

However, it is important to note that the theologians who took exception to parts of the Vatican instruction still expressed support of the Vatican's opposition to the use of surrogate mothers. The theologians were adamantly opposed to involving a third party in the reproductive process.

On March 10, 1987, the Vatican, in Rome, issued a new document that called for all governments to put strict limitations on medical interference in human procreation. The Roman Catholic Church called for laws prohibiting, among other things, surrogate mothers.

Even prior to the Vatican's announcement of its stand on the new reproductive technology, some Roman Catholic medical experts had already incorporated the Vatican's views into the medical practices of church-affiliated hospitals. Many church hospitals strongly discourage surrogate mothers bearing children for other couples from giving birth at their institutions. In fact, the Sisters of Bon Secours, which operates Catholic hospitals across the country, has passed a resolution to discourage surrogate mothers from having their babies delivered at the order's medical centers.

As Anne Neal, an ethicist with the hospitals, stated in the *New York Times*, "We thought we could do our little bit to discourage the whole surrogate arrangement by saying in advance that we choose not to, we prefer not to participate in the delivery. The group's hospitals would never turn away a woman who was a surrogate nor would they inquire into the nature of each birth, but officials hope instead that doctors will respect the hospital's views. In any case, Bon Secours hospitals would deal only with the mother on questions of medical care or payment for services, and would release the baby only to its mother."[9]

Non-Catholic hospitals with staffs and programs involved in advanced fertilization techniques have given little if any indication that they will comply with the Vatican guidelines. A number of these institutions permit surrogate mothers to be discharged from the hospital prior to the infant's release, to enable the adoptive parents to take the baby home themselves.

As Ewa Iradwanska, a physician at Rush Presbyterian St. Luke's Medical Center in Chicago, said of the hospital's in vitro fertilization program, "Since we started this program, I have never had any reason to think that there is anything inappropriate in it. And I'm certainly supported by my patients who say, 'If the process works, it must certainly be God's will.' "[10]

6
The Case of Baby M

In January 1985, twenty-seven-year-old Mary Beth Whitehead, a homemaker from Brick Township, New Jersey, and her thirty-seven-year-old husband, Richard, met with Dr. Elizabeth Stern, a pediatrician, and her husband, William, a biochemist. The two couples met for dinner at a restaurant in New Brunswick, New Jersey, approximately halfway between both their homes.

The meeting meant more than just an ordinary social engagement for everyone involved. Already a mother of a young son and daughter, Mary Beth Whitehead had decided to become pregnant again. But this time she had decided to become a surrogate mother and bear a baby to be surrendered to another couple immediately following its birth. That couple was to be William and Elizabeth Stern.

Mrs. Whitehead had referred to becoming a surrogate mother as offering a childless couple "the most loving gift of happiness." However, she was also aware of the monetary rewards involved, and she had hoped to use her surrogate mother's fee to pay for her children's higher education.

That night over dinner, the Sterns explained to the Whiteheads that due to a particular medical condition, a pregnancy could endanger Elizabeth Stern's health. Both couples discussed their reactions to and feelings about surrogate mother agreements. By the time the foursome had finished dining, the Sterns had chosen Mary Beth Whitehead to act as their child's surrogate mother. To cement their agreement, on February 6, 1985, both couples signed a contract negotiated by lawyer Noel Keane, who had brought the Sterns and the Whiteheads together. Keane had arranged more than one hundred and forty surrogate mother births since 1976.

The contract stated that the Sterns would pay $10,000 to Mary Beth Whitehead in addition to more than another $10,000 for fees and expenses associated with the birth. Mary Beth Whitehead was to be artificially inseminated with William Stern's sperm. The $10,000 to be paid to her was to be held in the attorney's escrow account until after the infant was born and the Sterns had obtained legal custody of the baby.

In addition, the contract between the Sterns and Mary Beth Whitehead specified that the Sterns would be legally responsible for the infant even if the child were born with serious mental or physical defects. During the pregnancy, Mrs. Whitehead was to undergo amniocentesis, a medical test to determine if the fetus would be born with certain genetic defects. If the test results were unfavorable, Mrs. Whitehead had agreed to have an abortion if that was what the Sterns wanted. According to the contract, the Whiteheads were clearly obligated to surrender the baby to the Sterns. Mrs. Whitehead contractually acknowledged that conception was to occur "for the sole purpose of giving said child to William Stern."

The first attempt at artificial insemination was conducted at a sperm bank in New York City. It was unsuccessful. On numerous occasions during the following months, Mr. Stern and Mrs. Whitehead would drive together from New Jersey to New York to repeat the effort. At times, they were accompanied by William Stern's wife, Elizabeth.

Finally, on July 2, 1985, Mary Beth Whitehead conceived. In *Newsweek*, William Stern described his reaction to hearing of the success. "I was stuck in Denver because of thunderstorms. I called Betsy to say I would be delayed. She told me that she had decorated the bathroom with streamers, pink and blue streamers. I did not catch on to what she was talking about. 'Don't you understand?' she asked. All of a sudden it dawned on me."[1] Later on his flight home, William Stern proudly told the passenger in the seat next to his, "I'm going to be a father."

Perhaps the early stages of Mary Beth Whitehead's pregnancy marked a high point in the relationship that subsequently ensued between the Sterns and the Whiteheads. Elizabeth Stern later recalled how she had initially enjoyed talking to Mary Beth, and how at the time Mary Beth Whitehead had seemed like a sister to her.

Physically, the women somewhat resembled one another. Both were slim and attractive, and wore their dark brown hair cut into bangs and falling softly against their high cheekbones. Both were said to have captivating smiles. Yet, in many ways, the two women had led very different lives.

Elizabeth Stern had studied for a number of years to become a doctor, a pediatrician. While having no biological children of her own, she had become expert at attending to the health needs of other people's children. She and her husband had gone through graduate school together, after which they had embarked on careers in the sciences.

Mary Beth Whitehead's life, on the other hand, had

Surrogate mother Mary Beth Whitehead, mother of Baby M

taken a dramatically different turn. She was a housewife who had dropped out of high school at sixteen to marry Richard Whitehead, a young man she had met while working as a waitress at a luncheonette.

Things had not always gone smoothly for the Whiteheads, who are the parents of two children, a daughter, Tuesday, now age ten, and a boy, Ryan, age twelve. They had weathered some difficult financial periods. In 1978, Mary Beth Whitehead was even on welfare for a time. Richard Whitehead, who is now employed as a sanitation worker, was once arrested for possession of marijuana. He also admitted to being an alcoholic, although he now claims that he has the problem under control.

The differences in the couples' backgrounds seemed to matter little at first. The Sterns and the Whiteheads had one crucial goal in common—the creation of a child for William and Elizabeth Stern. In the beginning, nothing else seemed important. They had started out as friends on a joint venture.

However, before long, uneasy feelings began to interrupt the couples' initially smooth relationship. Although Mrs. Whitehead seemed to have enjoyed William Stern's company on their frequent trips from their New Jersey homes to the New York sperm bank, Mr. Stern sensed that after she conceived, she seemed to withdraw from him.

Before long, friction between the two women also developed. Being a physician, Elizabeth Stern began to advise both Mrs. Whitehead and Mrs. Whitehead's doctor as to what would be best for the surrogate mother's health. She also insisted that Mary Beth go through with amniocentesis, against her own obstetrician's advice. She even took the liberty of calling Mrs. Whitehead's doctor to suggest that he prescribe a specific medication for the woman. Before long, Mary Beth Whitehead began to feel as though the Sterns were trying to take over her life.

Meanwhile, Mrs. Whitehead's own feelings about the baby she was carrying, as well as about the surrogacy agreement, began to change. As the fetus continued to grow inside of her, her doubts heightened. Mrs. Whitehead's mother stated in a *New York Times Magazine* article that "even during the pregnancy Mary Beth had already begun to pull back, wishing that she had never gotten into this mess because she knew that it was going to end badly."[2]

Near the end of the pregnancy, Mrs. Whitehead asked the Sterns if she'd be permitted to visit the child. The Sterns agreed, providing that the surrogate mother in no way revealed her true relationship to the child, but instead posed as a family friend or acquaintance. At the same time, Mary Beth Whitehead's husband, Richard, began to feel uncomfortable about the contractual agreement his wife had entered into. In *Newsweek*, he stated that he was troubled by "the thought of taking $10,000 for Ryan and Tuesday by selling their sister."[3]

The Whiteheads hadn't anticipated the emotions they were now experiencing over the baby Mrs. Whitehead was carrying. In fact, when she was eighteen, Mary Beth Whitehead had already decided that she didn't want any more children. She had even planned to have a tubal ligation to prevent further pregnancies, but after learning of the surgical details involved in the procedure, she decided against it. Instead, her husband, Richard, had a vasectomy.

When Mrs. Whitehead wanted to become a surrogate mother nine years later, at first her husband was against it. He referred to the surrogate agreement as a "weird idea." However, in time, he overcame his initial resistance to the idea, and proved extremely supportive of his wife's actions.

The doubts about surrendering the baby to the Sterns firmly crystallized with the infant's birth. Once the baby girl was delivered on March 27, 1986, Mary

Beth Whitehead realized that she had made a terrible mistake. She didn't want to be separated from her daughter and felt unable to give the baby to the Sterns. Her first moments alone with the child were intensely emotional. As Mrs. Whitehead recalled: "Seeing her, holding her . . . she was my child. It overpowered me. I had no control. I had to keep her."[4]

Trying to fight her own feelings, Mary Beth Whitehead did give her baby to the Sterns. But she found her first night without the child was torture. The following morning, she called the Sterns to beg them to allow her to keep the baby for only one week. They agreed, but when the week ended, Mrs. Whitehead still felt unable to return her daughter to them.

Mrs. Whitehead then proposed a sort of shared custody plan to the Sterns. She would allow the child to live with the Sterns, but she wanted her daughter to remain with her for at least one weekend during the month and for two weeks in the summer. The Sterns wanted no part of such an arrangement, and repeatedly insisted that Mary Beth Whitehead adhere to the terms of the original contract.

The Sterns went to court to attempt to have the contract legally enforced and to regain custody of the child. Meanwhile, the $10,000 Mary Beth Whitehead was to have been paid for her services as a surrogate mother remained in the escrow account. On May 5, a Bergen County Family Court judge awarded temporary custody of the infant to William and Elizabeth Stern.

The following day, police officers arrived at the Whitehead home armed with the court order. The police had intended to remove the child from the Whitehead residence. However, Mrs. Whitehead thwarted their efforts by passing the baby to her husband through an open window at the back of their house. The following day, the entire Whitehead family fled to Florida.

Mary Beth Whitehead, along with her husband, two

older children, and the baby, hid out in Florida for eighty-seven days, all the while attempting to evade both the law and the Sterns. The surrogate mother had wanted to keep her baby badly enough to cause her husband to leave his job as well as uproot her whole family. Her flight to escape with her daughter was severely limited, due to lack of funds. For while the Whiteheads hid out in Florida, the court had frozen Mrs. Whitehead's assets and placed a lien on her home to prevent its sale.

William and Elizabeth Stern spent over $20,000 on a private investigator in order to find the infant. Three months later, the baby and the Whitehead family were discovered at Mary Beth's mother's house in Holiday, Florida. The Whiteheads' older daughter Tuesday was there the day the private investigator, accompanied by FBI men, came to take the baby back to New Jersey.

The young girl's reaction to their intrusion was reported in *Newsweek*: "I heard a strange man's voice. I ran out of the bathroom to see what was going on. [There were] three men in the hallway in front of my sister's room. They saw the crib immediately, grabbed my sister, and ran out the front door. I screamed and said 'No.' I beat the back of the man who was holding the door with my hairbrush. They did not look back."[5]

The baby was brought back to live with the Sterns until a court of law could determine who would retain permanent custody of the infant. In the meantime, the Sterns began to feel very much like a family with a new baby. Each morning William Stern would rise at 5:00 A.M. to feed his daughter and play with her. Then he'd wake his wife to care for the child for the duration of the day.

Mary Beth Whitehead was permitted to visit the baby at the county office building for two-hour visits twice weekly. On August 13, 1986, Judge Harvey R. Sorkow of Superior Court in Hackensack, New Jersey, named Lorraine A. Abraham as the baby's legal guardian while the infant remained in the Sterns' temporary custody.

Finally, on January 5, 1987, the trial to determine the baby's legal parents began. One of the most publicized trials ever held, the case lasted for nearly two months, and became known throughout the country as the Baby M trial. The Sterns had named the baby Melissa. The Whiteheads called her Sara.

Referring to the infant as Baby M was a tactic thought up by one of the Sterns' lawyers, Edward J. O'Donnell, as a means of protecting the child's identity. It was reported in the *New York Times* that Mr. O'Donnell's first choice of a pseudonym for the baby had been Ann. He had thought of Ann based on the procedure meteorologists used in naming hurricanes, selecting names or labels for the storms in alphabetical order. However, the lawyer said that he later rejected the idea as inappropriate, since, "I didn't want to equate the child with a disaster."[6]

Many who watched the seven-week trial unfold felt that the proceedings often proved to be stormy and emotionally tumultuous. Much of Mary Beth Whitehead's present and past life were scrutinized and attacked by the Sterns' legal team. The differences in the backgrounds of the two couples were sharply accentuated. In fact, the Baby M case was often referred to as essentially "a matter of class."

The battling casts of characters were decidedly different. The Whiteheads' lawyers contended that the pair's social status was a built-in exploitation factor in the surrogate contract, because couples hiring surrogates will always be more affluent.

Harold J. Cassidy, representing the Whiteheads, stressed to the court that the roles could never be reversed. He insinuated that it would be extremely unlikely to find a successful and affluent young female doctor willing to take time out to bear a child for people in lower income brackets.

On the other side of the bitter custody battle remained William and Elizabeth Stern, professionals with graduate degrees, residing in the upscale suburban community of Tenafly, New Jersey. Forty-one-year-old Dr. Elizabeth Stern had put off child-rearing in order to pursue a career in medicine. She became a pediatrician in 1981, and also served as an assistant professor of pediatrics at the Albert Einstein College of Medicine in New York City.

In addition, Dr. Stern also holds a doctorate in human genetics. She has a mild case of multiple sclerosis, which she had diagnosed herself, although her diagnosis was later confirmed by other physicians. Because of her condition, she feared that becoming pregnant might worsen her health.

Gary M. Skoloff, representing the Sterns, had attempted to play down the differences in income by claiming that they were not so divergent. Richard Whitehead earns about $30,000 annually as a sanitation worker, while his wife is a homemaker. William Stern, a forty-one-year-old biochemist, earns $43,000, while his wife earns approximately $47,000 a year. However, since being awarded temporary custody of the baby, Dr. Stern has remained at home with the infant. She had indicated that she would later like to return to work part-time.

Skoloff tried to steer the case away from the class issue. He continually stressed that the only question at hand was that of determining which set of adults was better fit to raise the baby.

Once on the witness stand during the trial, both families displayed differences in their lives and in their plans for the child. William Stern said that he would like his daughter to attend college and would also encourage her to learn to play a musical instrument.

*William Stern,
Baby M's father*

Even before the baby had reached her first birthday, the Sterns had already taken her to the Museum of Natural History, an antique toy show, and a model railroad show.

Mrs. Whitehead testified that her husband liked to go fishing and crabbing with their twelve-year-old son, Ryan. Ryan and Tuesday both enjoyed sports, she added, and were actively involved in recreational soccer leagues.

When questioned on the witness stand about her qualifications to raise a baby, Mary Beth Whitehead replied, "I don't have an education. I don't have a skill. The only skill that I know I do well is being a mother. There's no limit to anything I'll do for my child."[7]

The personalities and tactics of the chief attorneys on the two sides were as diverse as their clients. The Sterns' principal lawyer, Gary M. Skoloff, had tried to create the perception that the baby's biological mother was an unreliable "liar," in order to counter any positive testimony she might offer.

To do so, he persistently attacked Mrs. Whitehead's emotional, financial, and marital stability, claiming that he wished to expose a "tremendous credibility gap" in Mrs. Whitehead's suitability as a parent. Mr. Skoloff described this tactic as giving "the judge great pause to think about the things they're saying. Each doubt leads to another doubt."[8]

On the other hand, Harold J. Cassidy, Mrs. Whitehead's chief attorney, had refused to launch a comparable counterattack on the Sterns. As Mr. Cassidy commented, "I don't believe throwing mud for the sake of throwing mud has any place in the court of law."[9]

Mr. Cassidy, who has described the use of surrogates as a "terrible practice," had framed his case as a defense of motherhood, and he sought to show that the forced separation of mother and child would lead to emotional trauma for both. Mr. Cassidy described surrogate motherhood as having "so much potential harm that it shouldn't even be considered by rational people." Throughout the trial, Mr. Cassidy sought professional opinions to confirm his argument.

However, Cassidy's emphasis on the emotional harm that might befall both Mrs. Whitehead and her daughter if they remained separated was repeatedly challenged from the bench by Judge Sorkow. The judge stated that this case was solely about what was in the *baby's* best interests. He stressed that the interests of Mrs. Whitehead, Mr. Stern, their respective spouses, or the needs of the baby's half-siblings were not the court's concern.

The testimony heard in court offered mixed reviews of Mary Beth Whitehead's parenting skills. Her lawyer had publicly stated that he'd be proud to be the parent of either Ryan or Tuesday Whitehead, and he had referred to the children as "proof of the pudding" with regard to Mrs. Whitehead's ability as a mother. In addition, several of the Whiteheads' neighbors, who had been interviewed by the county as part of the custody investigation, said that although they disagreed with Mrs. Whitehead's decision to keep the baby, they felt compelled to praise her superior mothering skills.

Some of the experts called in to assess the Whiteheads' home environment were not as kind. Three of the experts retained by the baby's court-appointed guardian claimed that they detected problems with the way in which Mrs. Whitehead interacted with her children. The experts, a clinical social worker, a psychiatrist, and a psychologist, found the children to exhibit signs of Mrs. Whitehead's over-protectiveness. Before answering questions, the children looked to their mother, the experts noted. The Whiteheads' lawyers criticized the report as assuming too much from nervous behavior exhibited by the children in a tense trial situation.

Dr. Lee Salk, a prominent author and pediatric psychology professor at Cornell University Medical College, testified that William Stern would be a more capable parent than Mary Beth Whitehead. The child psychologist recommended that William Stern and his wife be given permanent custody of the child, and that Mrs. Whitehead's parental rights be terminated. If this step were taken, Mary Beth Whitehead would permanently lose her right to ever see her daughter again. Dr. Salk did suggest that the two could meet later in life if that was what the child desired.

It is important to note that Dr. Salk testified at the Baby M trial on the Sterns' behalf and was paid $5,000 by the couple for his testimony. Dr. Salk had never met Mary Beth Whitehead personally, but had instead based his opinion on reports submitted by other experts involved in the case.

In addition, Dr. Salk has frequently been referred

One of the witnesses to testify on behalf of William and Elizabeth Stern in the Baby M custody trial was Dr. Lee Salk, prominent child psychologist.

to as a champion of father's rights. He himself was involved in a highly publicized custody dispute with his former wife, out of which he won custody of his own two children.

Among the reports cited by Dr. Salk was one submitted by Dr. Marshall D. Schechter, professor emeritus at the University of Pennsylvania School of Medicine in Philadelphia, who testified for Lorraine Abraham, Baby M's court-appointed guardian. Dr. Schechter diagnosed Mrs. Whitehead as suffering from a mental disability defined as a mixed personality disorder. However, when Ms. Abraham asked Dr. Schechter if Mary Beth Whitehead was an unfit mother, he replied, "No, she isn't."[10]

None of the other mental health experts in the hearing agreed with Dr. Schechter's diagnosis that Mary

Beth Whitehead had a mental disability, including Dr. David M. Brodzinsky, the legal guardian's other expert, or the two experts retained by the Sterns' legal staff.[11]

To strengthen their case against the Whiteheads, the Sterns' legal team continually focused attention on the fact that Mrs. Whitehead's husband, Richard, had been known to have a drinking problem. In response, Richard Whitehead took exception to the implications made to his drinking during the trial. According to Mr. Whitehead, he does not mind collecting garbage for a living, but resents now being known as "the alcoholic garbage man." Mr. Whitehead blames his negative portrayal on the Sterns.

As Richard Whitehead told the *Asbury Park Press*, "Elizabeth Stern told us last May that she would drag us through the mud unless we stopped our battle for Sara. She is certainly living up to her promise. I think the whole country knows me as the alcoholic trash man. It bothers me a lot. But this public picture has been painted of me and it seems I'm stuck with it."[12]

Mr. Whitehead feels that he now has his drinking problem under control.

It's very hard, but I've been saying no to alcohol. I think part of it is realizing that you have a problem. For a long time I denied the whole thing. Instead of concentrating on my alcohol problems, I think it would be fairer if the Sterns' lawyers brought out what a loving family we are.

. . . I know Mary for fourteen years, and believe me, I would know if she had split personalities. She's the most loving mother in the world. She devotes her whole life to those kids. It hurts me to see her attacked like this. It annoys me so much what the Sterns are doing.

I was in the delivery [room] when Sara was born,

> and when I first looked at her I realized that she looked like Tuesday [one of the Whitehead children]. It was then that both Mary and I realized that we had made a mistake. Sara is part of our family. I'm not going to give up on her.[13]

Little—if any—of the Whiteheads' family life was allowed to remain private throughout the trial. Not only did the Sterns' lawyers bring up Richard Whitehead's problems, but the surrogate mother was forced to speak about it herself, in explaining why she took a job as a go-go dancer to support the family after her husband was arrested for drunken driving. Witnesses were called to discuss the school record of Mrs. Whitehead's son, Ryan, and a counselor was forced to testify about a session with the Whitehead family.

The Sterns' lawyer had come armed with a police report on a marital spat, a bankruptcy petition made by the Whiteheads, and other documents dug out by private detectives. In Mr. Skoloff's cross-examination of Mrs. Whitehead, he continually pressed for further details on the negative elements in her background.

At one point during cross-examination, Mary Beth Whitehead revealed that she had paid up to date on the first mortgage of her house—which was in foreclosure—with a loan through her lawyer, Harold J. Cassidy. She settled eight months of $390-a-month payments for her Brick Township home with a loan from a real estate firm in which her attorney Cassidy is a principal, she testified.

It soon became clear that the vicious and drawn-out battle for Baby M had taken its toll on the Whiteheads. Richard Whitehead, already tall and thin, began to look exceedingly worn and weary. Mary Beth Whitehead's weight dropped from 140 pounds to 110 pounds.

At several points during the trial, raw emotions surfaced. This became especially apparent when two chilling, taped telephone conversations between William Stern and Mary Beth Whitehead were played in court. The first tape was made by Stern on July 15, 1986, as he sat at his desk at work. His lawyer had advised him to tape all phone conversations pertaining to the case.

This conversation took place two weeks before William Stern had obtained possession of his daughter, after the Whiteheads' Florida flight. These words were spoken before the world had ever heard of Baby M.

> Mrs. Whitehead: *This is not fair, Bill. You have me so emotionally upset. [crying, nearly hysterically]*
> Stern: *Mary Beth . . .*
> Mrs. Whitehead: *And how about the baby? I'm caring for her.*
> Stern: *Mary Beth, calm down, please.*
> Mrs. Whitehead: *You really care.*
> Stern: *I care about her. I don't . . . I want her, Mary Beth. I want my child.*
> Mrs. Whitehead: *And I do too.*
> Stern: *Then what do we do, Mary Beth?*
> Mrs. Whitehead: *That's exactly it, Bill. What do we do, go to see fancy lawyers and go to judges? Is it really going to make a difference? Bill, I can't live without her.*
> Stern: *Mary Beth . . .*
> Mrs. Whitehead: *She can't live without me. I have no money and me and Sara are living in hiding. Isn't that a nice way for your daughter to live?*
> Stern: *No, it's not a nice way for my daughter to live.*
> Mrs. Whitehead: *Yep, you don't care. I'll tell her, I'll tell her exactly what happened. I'm not going to be still. I'm going to tell her exactly what happened when she's eighteen years old, and I'll tell it honestly.*

Still later in the conversation Mrs. Whitehead said, "I can't do it, Bill. I'd rather be dead than give her up."

"How would my daughter feel if I didn't fight for her?" Stern asked.

"How do you think she would feel about me if I didn't fight for her?" Mrs. Whitehead asked.

As the tape continued, Mrs. Whitehead asked in anguish, "You want me to kill myself and the baby? I gave her life, I can take her life away."

"No," replied Stern. "That's why I gave her to you in the first place, because I didn't want you to kill yourself."

During their conversation, Stern also brought up the intent of the original contract that had existed between them. "You made an agreement," he said.

"Aren't I allowed to change my mind?" Mrs. Whitehead asked.

"You don't change your mind about things like this, Mary Beth, that's what courts are all about. I want my daughter back," Stern replied.

"Forget it, Bill," Mrs. Whitehead said angrily. "I'll tell you right now, I'd rather see her and me dead before you get her."

Stern pleaded: "Don't, Mary Beth, don't."[14] At various times during the taped conversation, Baby M could be heard crying in the background.

Mrs. Whitehead was not the only one to show emotion. Stern, although steadier throughout, faltered at times. Several times during the conversation, he said, "Oh, God," and became frantic near the end of the forty-five-minute tape when Mrs. Whitehead threatened to take his daughter's life.

On a second tape made the following day, Mrs. Whitehead threatened to accuse William Stern of molesting her young daughter Tuesday, while driving the girl home after an outing with the Sterns. Mrs. Whitehead later admitted to reporters that the threatened child molestation charge was actually nothing more than "a tactic I was using to make [Stern] stop hurting me and my family."[15]

The tapes were heard in the Hackensack, New Jersey, courtroom, to bolster William and Elizabeth Stern's claim that Mary Beth Whitehead was emotionally unstable and that they should be awarded permanent custody of the child. As the tape played, Mrs. Whitehead wiped tears from her eyes, and Stern appeared visibly shaken.

Some observers felt that Mrs. Whitehead's taped threats to harm the infant girl were among the most damaging evidence against her. Dr. David M. Brodzinsky, one of the court-appointed guardian's psychological experts, characterized Mrs. Whitehead's comments to William Stern as being "manipulative and directed at forcing Mr. Stern to lift a freeze he had obtained on her assets. . . . Mrs. Whitehead was in control of the conversation . . . suicidal people lack the capacity to manipulate others and control conversations." On February 23, 1987, Dr. Brodzinsky said to reporters in a statement out of court, "I don't believe she was suicidal *or* homicidal."[16]

William and Elizabeth Stern's three-member legal team continued to present a skillful, intense attack on Mary Beth Whitehead and her family. Repeatedly, throughout the non-jury hearing, Mrs. Whitehead had been referred to as a liar and a manipulator, and was characterized as being both suicidal and homicidal.

The Sterns' chief lawyer so routinely raised this negative perception of Mrs. Whitehead—in motions, in court filings, and in his own questioning—that it wasn't difficult to lose sight of the fact that few of the mental health experts who testified agreed with it.

Since the judge had refused to consider the psychological harm to Mrs. Whitehead that might result from the loss of her daughter, only the question of how the baby might be emotionally scarred could be considered

William Stern and Baby M

relevant to the proceedings. The Sterns' legal team asserted that the baby's potential insecurities about her origins and separation from her birth mother could be reduced by the Sterns if they depicted Mrs. Whitehead as a kind person who, in generosity, bore them a child.

However, Dr. Steven L. Nickman of Harvard Medical School, one of the Whiteheads' psychiatric experts, testified that children born of surrogate agreements risk psychological harm. His opinion was further supported by still another expert witness for the Whiteheads, Dr. Burton Z. Sokoloff, who asserted that a forced separation could have lasting effects on the baby as well as on Mrs. Whitehead and her family.

Phyllis R. Silverman, a psychiatric social worker, testified at the Baby M trial that women cannot realize the full impact of signing away a child before it is born. In addition, Mrs. Whitehead's chief lawyer argued that his client's constitutional rights would be violated if the court terminated her parental rights without showing neglect or abuse.

The Sterns' attorneys had attempted to discredit the testimony of Whitehead's experts by claiming that their conclusions were only based on comparable or analogous situations, such as the experiences of adoptees. They had argued early on in the case that witnesses should not be allowed to testify on the potential damage to a mother or child in surrogate agreements, because not enough is known about the subject for anyone to qualify as an expert.

In response, Cassidy claimed that efforts to discredit witnesses who had not had direct experience with surrogate arrangements were a disservice to the court. He argued that it was fitting to draw conclusions from similar experiences.

Mrs. Whitehead was to experience further setbacks during the trial. At one point, Susan Hergenhan, Mrs. Whitehead's former backyard neighbor and perhaps her best character witness, admitted lying under oath and signing Mrs. Whitehead's name to an emotional eleven-page plea to Judge Sorkow in May 1987.

Thirty-five-year-old Susan Hergenhan acknowledged that she was the author of a handwritten May 18th letter that attacked William and Elizabeth Stern, countered their court charges, and dramatically detailed the Whitehead's side of the story. Hergenhan also admitted that she had lied in her earlier testimony when she denied ever having seen court documents. The documents were sent to her home by the Sterns' lawyers for Whitehead, who had fled with the baby. Hergenhan said that she passed the documents on to Whitehead's sister-in-law.

In an effort to clear up matters, Mary Beth Whitehead said on the witness stand that she had spoken about the letter to Hergenhan, who lived in a house next door to the Whiteheads in Brick Township until July 1986. "I've never seen it," Whitehead said. "But I can explain it. I just talked to Sue Hergenhan and she wrote it in my behalf. She just told me."[17]

Whitehead said that Hergenhan also wrote a letter to the judge under her own name. Mrs. Whitehead described her friend as having information which "I had relayed to her" in the event that she wrote a letter. Whitehead said that she knew that Hergenhan had planned to write, but that she never saw the finished letter.

The handwritten letter, which was originally believed to be the court's first communication from Whitehead, related past incidents between the Whiteheads and the Sterns in shocking detail, and had been purported by the press to reveal Mary Beth Whitehead's innermost feelings.

The document, supposedly written by Mrs. Whitehead herself, read: "I became unglued when I saw my baby going off with them. I cried for hours and lay awake all night, pining for my baby. I felt I had made a terrible decision in giving her to them."[18]

The letter directly countered allegations made by

the Sterns in their court papers, such as charges that Mary Beth Whitehead might have been mixing alcohol and Valium, or had been suicidal. It also accused Dr. Elizabeth Stern of not wanting to have a baby for career reasons. The letter continued, "The way in which the matter was handled absolutely left us feeling helpless and trapped. We had no alternative than to do what we did."[19]

Gary M. Skoloff, the Sterns' attorney, said outside court that the forgery was a "complete shock to everybody." Skoloff contended that it cast doubt on the credibility of all of Whitehead's friends who testified, as well as on Mary Beth Whitehead herself. He said, "It's another item in the mosaic of the credibility of Mary Beth Whitehead."

Towards the end of the trial, Baby M's court-appointed guardian attorney made her recommendations to the judge as to what action the court should take. As the child's guardian, Mrs. Abraham was the child's advocate only, and theoretically impartial. In her trial summation, Mrs. Abraham suggested that the parental rights of Mary Beth Whitehead be retained, although custody of the eleven-month-old-girl should be permanently awarded to the infant's father, William Stern, and his wife, Elizabeth.

If Mary Beth Whitehead's parental rights were terminated by the court, she would forfeit all her rights as the baby's mother, including that of ever being permitted to see her daughter again. Mrs. Abraham stated to the court that ending Mrs. Whitehead's rights would be "irrevocable" and "inhuman." The court-appointed guardian added that she was against ending Mrs. Whitehead's parental rights, since at this time it was difficult to predict the child's future need or desire to have personal contact with her biological mother.

As Mrs. Abraham stated to the presiding judge, "Termination now is so awesome a step that we cannot, in all conscience, take it. We are not omniscient."[20]

7
Baby M—
Whose Child Is She?

Both those in favor of and against surrogate parenting regarded the termination of parental rights as the pivotal issue in the seven-week landmark trial of Baby M. In fact, the termination of Mrs. Whitehead's parental rights was the key provision in the original surrogate contract signed by both Mary Beth Whitehead and William Stern. Mr. Stern initiated the court action both to gain permanent custody of his daughter and to petition that the court uphold the provision in order to enable his wife to legally adopt Baby M.

Gary M. Skoloff, the Sterns' chief lawyer expressed disappointment in Mrs. Abraham's recommendation to the court, in that he felt it might lead to further bouts of litigation between the Whiteheads and the Sterns. He also expressed concern that not terminating Mrs. Whitehead's parental rights might serve to confuse the little girl about her parents.

As Mr. Skoloff stated in his one hour and forty minute summation, "Total termination affords the baby her only chance—her only chance—to achieve this peace and stability. . . . If ever there was a case where some adult has to lose if a baby is to win, this is that case. If ever there was a case where a court must fashion a remedy to save a child, this is it."[1]

The court summations also included an appeal from Mrs. Whitehead's parents (Baby M's grandparents). Joseph Messer, a sixty-six-year-old retired school teacher, and his wife, Catherine, a sixty-five-year-old mother of eight, pleaded that visitation rights be granted to them as the baby's grandparents. The Messers' attorney argued that New Jersey state law permits grandparents to visit their grandchildren in instances in which a child's parents were divorced, living apart, or dead.

The Messers' attorney described the couple as loving, hard-working people. He told the court that, "All their loving characteristics and good qualities would somehow be communicated to Baby M." Mrs. Abraham requested that the judge grant the infant's grandparents visitation rights, but she stressed that the visits from the child's grandmother and grandfather should only take place in the Sterns' home and on their terms.

The Sterns' lawyers argued against visitation rights for Mrs. Whitehead's parents. They pointed out to the court that the Messers had helped Mary Beth Whitehead hide from the law when she took Baby M and fled to Florida.

On the day the court summations from both sides were heard, a group of women demonstrated outside the courthouse during the noon recess in support of Mary Beth Whitehead. The supporters carried signs bearing slogans such as "Sara Whitehead is her name," "Sara is a little sister," and "Mothers With Feelings." The demonstrators distributed a statement signed by over one hundred prominent women which read, "We strongly urge the legislators and jurists who deal with these matters to recognize that a mother need not be perfect to deserve her child."

Inside the courtroom, Mary Beth Whitehead's law-

Demonstrators supporting Mary Beth Whitehead outside the Hackensack, New Jersey courthouse during the trial. Ms. Whitehead is second from the left.

yer seemed to echo the demonstrators' sentiments as he said, "It will always be the wife of the sanitation worker who must bear the children of the pediatrician. We must never permit a man to have one woman share his life and another to experience the sacrifice and pain of pregnancy."[2]

On numerous other occasions throughout the trial, feminists and other protestors had gathered outside the courthouse to voice their support for Mary Beth Whitehead. At one point, as Elizabeth Stern returned to the courtroom from lunch, the demonstrators screamed "baby stealer" at her. Although the Sterns' attorneys characterized the protests as "inappropriate," Mrs. Stern's only comment had been, "They're entitled to their opinion."

The closing arguments of the lawyers for both sides served to underscore the way in which the two sides viewed the original surrogate agreement's validity. Mr. Skoloff argued that both the Sterns and Mrs. Whitehead understood the terms of the agreement, and that Mary Beth Whitehead had no right to go back on her part of the arrangement.

Mrs. Whitehead's lawyer argued that the stipulation in the surrogate mother agreement that forced a woman to surrender her parental rights before conception was contrary to state law. Mr. Cassidy claimed that those terms violated the state adoption laws, which permit women a grace period after their child's birth in which to determine if they still wish to surrender the child.

Cassidy continued his argument, stating that Dr. Elizabeth Stern should be prohibited by law from adopting Baby M, since Mary Beth Whitehead was already the girl's mother, and there was no evidence that Mrs. Whitehead had ever abused, neglected, or abandoned her daughter. The court-appointed guardian seemed to agree with Cassidy's reasoning on this point, as she stated to the judge in her summation, "Present state law does not allow the court to permit termination [of Mrs. Whitehead's maternal rights]."

The Sterns' lawyer countered their contention, stating that adoption law wasn't relevant to the case. He stressed that surrogate agreements were relatively new arrangements and, as such, needed to be viewed as an entirely different matter.

As the now-famous trial drew to a conclusion, the weight of the Baby M decision rested solely on Judge Sorkow's shoulders. The judge remained virtually silent throughout the trial's last day, refusing to take the traditional 10:30 A.M. break, and encouraging the attorneys to continue their closing arguments through lunch until the hearing finally came to a close at about 1:30 P.M.

The thrust of Cassidy's closing argument to the judge was an emotional appeal not to tear a baby from its mother's arms, but to instead declare the surrogate mother contract between Mary Beth Whitehead and the Sterns unenforceable. Cassidy began, "On March 27, 1986, in a flush of ecstasy which followed her giving birth to a new human being, Mary Beth Whitehead knew that she could not deny her motherhood. There in the delivery room of Monmouth Medical Center, Long Branch, she knew and felt that there was a bond between her and her child stronger than any sense of obligation she had to William Stern."[3]

The Sterns' lawyer also attempted to elicit sympathy from the judge, describing his clients as a childless couple who expected a child and were devastated when the Brick Township surrogate mother decided that she could not give the infant up. He stated to the court, "The Sterns joyfully prepared the baby's room. They were the expectant parents. At the Whitehead house there was no decorating. There was no crib."[4]

Judge Sorkow's response to the attorneys from both sides was, "Your presentations serve to further crystallize for the court its awesome burden."[5]

At a press conference immediately following the trial's end, the Sterns expressed relief that their long ordeal was finally over. Elizabeth Stern said that she and her husband were looking forward to resuming a normal life. Of the disagreement that existed between the two couples, William Stern said, "I have mixed feelings about the trial. On the one hand, I feel very bad about seeing Mary Beth and all that's happened to her. And I'm grateful to her for carrying such a beautiful child. On the other hand, I'm still angry at her for having gone to the press."[6]

Although Mrs. Whitehead and her husband were present for the trial's closing arguments, they declined to speak to reporters afterwards. Throughout her attorney's forty-five-minute summation, Mary Beth Whitehead cried softly. Her husband sat silently by her side, occasionally glancing blankly at the Sterns.

Attending the trial, in addition to those directly involved with the case, were a group of spectators who regularly arrived at the Bergen County Court House each day. Some were retired people, some were housewives, others were self-employed. Since there were only fourteen seats reserved for the public, they had to rise early each day to secure a place for themselves in the courtroom. Yet these individuals continued to sit regularly through most of the custody fight alongside reporters from all over the United States, Europe, and Asia.

"This is a building of sorrows," a self-employed design engineer from Tenafly, New Jersey, who declined to give his name, told the *Asbury Park Press*. "Everyone's problems are brought here for judication. You can almost feel it on the walls."[7] He and his wife had missed less than a handful of days in the trial. Although they had supported Mary Beth Whitehead when they first entered the courtroom, they had since switched sides. As the Tenafly engineer described his feelings, "I feel compassion for her, but all the testimony

The anguish of the natural mother, Mary Beth Whitehead, is evident as she is embraced by Elizabeth Kane, one of the first surrogate mothers.

with the Whiteheads raised an issue of credibility to me."[8]

Other spectators remained loyal to Mary Beth Whitehead. Among these was freelance writer Nora Johnson, who solemnly told a reporter, "They crucify her for running off to Florida when the police tried to take her baby. How could she do anything else? To me it shows that she's a good mother. It's natural instincts."[9]

Still other spectators experienced mixed feelings as they listened to the testimony given by both sides. As one woman said, "I'm wavering back and forth the whole time. Mary Beth has two children and the Sterns don't have any. I don't think that this whole surrogate mother thing should be outlawed, because sometimes there is a need. But I don't think that she should be faulted for not being able to give up the child, absolutely not."[10]

The final day of the hearing was among the more somber and peaceful days of the lengthy trial. It had been a trial marked by numerous confrontations between the attorneys representing the Sterns and the Whiteheads. Harold J. Cassidy made no secret of his feelings that a higher court might have to rectify a lower court's decision. Often Cassidy employed the word "ultimately" when referring to Mary Beth Whitehead's victory in the case. "Ultimately," the contract will be ruled void, he'd say, or "ultimately" the court will negate a ruling that completely cuts off either the infant's biological mother or father.

Later that month, on March 31st, Judge Sorkow delivered his long-awaited decision in the Baby M trial. The judge awarded custody to the baby's father, William Stern. In addition, he terminated all of Mary Beth Whitehead's parental rights. In his ruling, the judge arbitrarily negated the arguments put forth by Mrs. Whitehead's lawyer that the Stern–Whitehead surrogate agreement violated state adoption laws as well as statutes against baby selling.

In his decision, Judge Sorkow said that he was creating new law through this first case tried in a United States court between two parties over a surrogate mother contract. According to the judge, "Laws governing adoption, custody and ending paternal rights predate surrogate parenthood. To make a new concept fit into an old statute makes tortured law with equally tortured results."[11]

Judge Sorkow ruled in favor of the Sterns on all issues brought before the court. Claiming that state adoption laws "did not apply to surrogate contracts," Judge Sorkow stated, "The biological father pays the surrogate for her willingness to be impregnated and carry his child to term. At birth, the father does not purchase the child. It is his own biological, genetically related child. He cannot purchase what is already his. That bargain here was one for totally personal services."

The judge's ruling included a biting attack against Mary Beth Whitehead, in which he described her as being "manipulative," "repulsive," and "exploitative." He added that Mrs. Whitehead "has a genuine problem in recognizing and reporting the truth." Judge Sorkow described the Whitehead household as being "plagued with separations, domestic violence, and severe financial difficulties requiring household moves."

Judge Sorkow stated that he felt obligated to validate the surrogate mother agreement and to end Mrs. Whitehead's parental rights if he were to act in the child's "best interests." The judge said, "There can be no solution which is satisfactory to all in this kind of case. Justice, our desired object, to the child and the mother, to the child and the father, cannot be obtained for both parents. The court will seek to achieve justice for the child."

Judge Sorkow described the Whiteheads as giving "a reduced level of importance" to education, while he felt that the Sterns "show sensitivity to the child's physical and emotional needs. . . . They would initiate and encourage intellectual curiosity and learning for the child." The judge characterized the Sterns' marriage as "strong and mutually supportive."

In the final pages of his one-hundred-and-twenty-one-page decision, the judge referred to Baby M as Melissa, which was the name the Sterns had given her. Towards the end of the decision, the judge also denied a request by Mary Beth Whitehead's parents to be allowed to visit their grandchild. Judge Sorkow ended his written opinion by stating that Melissa needed no further lawsuits as well as "protection from anyone who would threaten her protection."

Mrs. Whitehead was not in court to hear the decision; she remained at her Brick Township home. Her lawyers said that she would appeal the decision against her.

Many who followed the Baby M case from the beginning seemed stunned by the scope and severity of Judge Sorkow's ruling. His decision to fully terminate Mrs. Whitehead's parental rights went far beyond the recommendations of Baby M's court-appointed legal guardian. Mrs. Abraham had argued that, under current state law, Judge Sorkow did not have grounds to end Mrs. Whitehead's maternal rights.

Apparently, the judge felt otherwise. What's more, if Judge Sorkow's ruling to terminate Mrs. Whitehead's parental rights are upheld, it would mean that Baby M's birth mother would have no legal authority to ever see her daughter again.

In his ruling on behalf of the Sterns, the judge heavily relied on the 1985 surrogate contract in which Mrs. Whitehead promised both to give up the baby and to willingly surrender her parental rights. As Judge Sorkow stated in his decision, "The contract is not illusory. Mrs. Whitehead was anxious to contract. This court finds that she has changed her mind, reneged on her promise, and now seeks to avoid her obligations."

Jeff Rosenburg, the director of public policy for the National Committee for Adoption, a group in opposition to surrogate mother agreements, said of Judge Sorkow's decision, "By saying surrogate parenthood agreements are enforceable, the judge is saying we can bind a woman to a preconception agreement to give up a child. And if she developed a natural attachment and decided she wanted to parent her flesh and blood, we should send the police in."[12]

Following the decision, William and Elizabeth Stern were met by a throng of reporters, television cameras, and spectators as they left the courthouse. Attempting to control his emotions, William Stern said of the judge's decision, "I have a tingling feeling in my elbows and my legs are numb. I'm so happy."[13]

At that point, Mr. Stern began to weep. He rested his head on his wife's shoulder and appeared unable to go on speaking. His wife continued for him, saying, "Bill and I are very very sorry that what started out as a very nice thing had to end up like this." When asked about her feelings regarding Mary Beth Whitehead, Elizabeth Stern replied, "She gave us a beautiful daughter."

However, Baby M's future was yet to be determined. On April 10, 1987, the New Jersey Supreme Court agreed to hear Mrs. Whitehead's appeal of Judge Sorkow's decision. Meanwhile, in the remaining months prior to the hearing, the Supreme Court allowed Mrs. Whitehead to visit her daughter for two hours each week.

On April 14th, Mary Beth Whitehead had a tearful reunion with her then thirteen-month-old daughter, whom she still calls Sara. It was the first time in two weeks that Mrs. Whitehead had been allowed to see her baby. The visit took place at a child care center in Hackensack, New Jersey, where for two hours Mrs. Whitehead lovingly hugged and kissed the baby as she gently rocked her young daughter in her arms. Mrs. Whitehead described her visit with her daughter to reporters: "I'm so happy. It was so great to be with her. I'm thrilled to see my child again."[14]

As soon as her visitation hours were up, Mary Beth Whitehead rushed out of the day care center and was driven away. Several moments later, a somber-looking William Stern came out of the day care center carrying Baby M. He then drove his daughter back to their home in Tenafly, New Jersey.

In August 1987, an additional brief was filed by the American Adoption Congress with the State Supreme Court. The brief argued that Mrs. Whitehead's ties to the baby ought not to be severed. According to the document, the Superior Court decision that terminated Mrs. Whitehead's parental rights "failed to understand the importance of preserving the full heritage of a child, including ties to both natural parents."[15]

The brief continues, stating that "like other adoptees, Baby M will be placed at psychological risk, because one of the major means through which individuals develop a secure sense of self is through identification with their parents. Identification with the parent of the same sex is particularly important."[16]

Although the Whiteheads tried to be supportive of one another, the bitter Baby M custody battle took its toll on their marriage. On November 12, 1987, Richard and Mary Beth Whitehead divorced. According to Mr. Whitehead's lawyer, "Pressures from the case were 95 percent responsible for the divorce. He was with her all the way, but it exhausted their marriage."[17]

Following the divorce, Mary Beth remarried. Her new husband is Dean Gould. Shortly after their marriage, the couple announced that Mary Beth was pregnant with their child.

On February 3, 1988, the New Jersey Supreme Court rendered its decision in the Baby M case. The court ruled that surrogate contracts are unenforceable, invalid, and perhaps even criminal in the state of New Jersey. The seven Supreme Court justices determined that paying women to bear children amounts to baby selling.

According to the Court, the only type of surrogate arrangement that may be considered valid is that in which no fee is paid to the surrogate and in which the biological mother has an opportunity to change her mind. In the event that the surrogate decides that she wants to keep her baby, the fact that she signed a contract becomes irrelevant. At that point, the determination of where the child will live becomes nothing more than a custody dispute.

The New Jersey Supreme Court awarded the Sterns permanent custody of Baby M. However, the court also overturned a ban on Mary Beth's visitation rights that had been ordered by the lower court. Although Baby M will continue to live with William and Elizabeth Stern, Mrs. Whitehead-Gould will be permitted to see her daughter. The decision to place the child with the Sterns was based on the Court's conclusion that the Sterns could offer the child a better quality of life.[18]

Experts say that at this time no one actually knows what psychological repercussions will result from Baby M's being born out of a surrogate agreement or from the bitter custody fight waged throughout the child's first years of life. Angela R. Holder, a professor of legal issues in pediatrics at Yale Medical School, stated in *The New York Times*, "I haven't heard any outpouring of people who think this might be a good thing. I think more people are against it than before. . . . The whole case is just a tragedy for the child, because of both the publicity and the litigation."[19]

A clinical professor of child psychiatry at Columbia University, Richard A. Gardner, echoed these sentiments, saying of the child, "For the rest of her life, she'll be the famous Baby M."[20]

Epilogue

Surrogate motherhood continues in America today, as does the controversy surrounding it. The famous Baby M case only served to underscore the urgent need for legislation to regulate the process as well as other forms of the new reproductive technology. Guidelines are essential in order to prevent subjecting the participants to the potential emotional and financial damage that can result from extensive litigation.

Although most states have not passed laws to regulate surrogacy, in July 1987, Louisiana became the first state to pass a law prohibiting surrogacy. In New Jersey, surrogate contracts in which the surrogate mother is paid a fee are unacceptable. Other states are considering the surrogacy matter. There is still no consensus as to what might work best. Proposed laws appear to reflect the many diverse reactions to surrogate motherhood itself.

For example, in New York, a proposed bill would permit binding surrogate mother contract agreements if they were approved by a family court judge, while in Connecticut another proposed law would prohibit payment to a surrogate mother except for medical expenses. A couple or individual who entered into such agreements illegally would lose the child to its biological mother in the event of a custody dispute.

A proposed Pennsylvania law would allow a surrogate mother twenty days after giving birth to determine if she wanted to keep the baby, while a Rhode Island proposal would automatically declare a surrogate mother contract void in the event of a custody dispute.

It's been argued that it's unfair to design laws to regulate surrogate motherhood without a full understanding of the long-term effects on the children involved. Some researchers have suggested that surrogate offspring might be devastated by the knowledge that their biological mother was paid to give birth to them, while others may feel that the love and caring of a supportive adoptive home would compensate for any potential problems inherent in the process.[1]

At this point, there are no clear-cut answers. As expressed in *Newsweek* by Daniel Callahan, director of the Hastings Center, "We are wandering into all kinds of new parental relationships. I don't think we have the faintest idea of how it's going to work out. It's a social experiment."[2]

Source Notes

Chapter 1
1. Noel P. Keane with Dennis L. Breo, *The Surrogate Mother* (New York: Everest House, 1981), 57–74.

Chapter 2
1. Lori B. Andrews, *New Conceptions: A Consumer's Guide to the Newest Infertility Treatments, Including In Vitro Fertilization, Artificial Insemination, and Surrogate Motherhood* (New York: St. Martin's Press, 1984), 123.
2. Ibid., p. 137.
3. Ibid., p. 181.
4. *People*, 19 October 1987, 42.
5. *Fortune*, 17 November 1984, 41.

Chapter 3
1. Hastings Center Report, New York, February 1987, 16–17.
2. *Time*, 10 September 1984, 54.
3. Hastings Center Report, August 1985, 67.

4. *Ms.*, December 1986, 42.
5. Ibid., p. 45.
6. *New York Times*, 1 April 1987, B2.
7. *People*, 13 June 1984, 49.
8. Ibid., p. 50.
9. *Time*, op. cit. 56.
10. Ibid., p. 56.

Chapter 4
1. *U.S. News & World Report*, 6 June 1983, 77.
2. *Omni*, June 1983, 22.
3. *Newsweek*, 19 January 1987, 47.
4. *U.S. News & World Report*, op. cit.
5. Ibid.
6. *Health*, April 1985, 65.
7. *Redbook*, April 1986, 34–38.
8. *Ladies Home Journal*, October 1985, 20.
9. Ibid.
10. *Time*, 19 January 1987, 58.
11. *Newsweek*, op. cit., p. 46.
12. Ibid.
13. *New York Times*, 2 March 1987, B4.
14. Ibid.
15. Ibid.
16. Ibid.
17. Ibid.

Chapter 5
1. *Time*, 10 September 1984, 54.
2. Ibid.
3. *New York Times* (*Magazine* section), 29 March 1987, 33.
4. *New York Times*, 1 April 1987, B2.
5. Ibid.
6. Ibid.
7. *New York Times*, 11 March 1987, 1.
8. Ibid.

9. Ibid., p. 17A.
10. Ibid.

Chapter 6
1. *Newsweek*, 19 January 1987, 48.
2. *New York Times*, (*Magazine* section), 29 March 1987, 87.
3. *Newsweek*, op. cit., p. 49.
4. Ibid.
5. Ibid.
6. *New York Times*, 9 February 1987, B3.
7. *New York Times*, 10 February 1987, B1.
8. *New York Times*, 23 February 1987, B1.
9. Ibid.
10. *New York Post*, 24 February 1987, 4.
11. *New York Times*, 25 February 1987, B2.
12. *Asbury Park Press*, 15 February 1987, A13.
13. *Asbury Park Press*, 18 February 1987, A14.
14. *New York Post*, 5 February 1987, 7.
15. Ibid.
16. *New York Times*, 3 March 1987, 37.
17. *Star Ledger* (Newark, New Jersey), 20 February 1987, 16.
18. Ibid.
19. Ibid.
20. *New York Times*, 1 April 1987, B3.

Chapter 7
1. *New York Times*, 13 March 1987, B3.
2. Ibid.
3. *Asbury Park Press*, 15 March 1987, 1.
4. Ibid., p. A4.
5. *Asbury Park Press*, 15 March 1987, 1.
6. Ibid., p. A4.
7. Ibid.
8. Ibid.
9. Ibid.

10. Ibid.
11. *New York Times*, 1 April 1987, 1.
12. Ibid., p. B3.
13. Ibid.
14. *New York Post*, 4 April 1987, 4.
15. *New York Times*, 5 August 1987, B1.
16. Ibid.
17. *New York Times*, 3 November 1987, B1.
18. *New York Post*, 3 February 1988, 5.
19. *New York Times*, 1 April 1987, B2.
20. Ibid.

Epilogue
1. *Newsweek*, 13 April 1987, 21.
2. Ibid., p. 22.

For Further Reading

BOOKS

Andrews, Lori B. *New Conceptions: A Consumer's Guide to the Newest Infertility Treatments.* New York: St. Martin's, 1984.

Keane, Noel P., with Dennis L. Breo. *The Surrogate Mother.* New York: Everest House, 1981.

Singer, Pete. *Making Babies: The New Science and Ethics of Conception.* New York: Scribner's, 1985.

Snyder, Gerald S. *Test-Tube Life: Scientific Advances and Moral Dilemma.* New York: Julian Messner, 1982.

ARTICLES

"After the Baby M Case: the debate over surrogacy has only begun," *Newsweek*, 13 April 1987, p. 22.

"Calling King Solomon—(Baby M)," *The New Republic*, vol. 196, 23 February 1987, p. 9.

"How Surrogates Are Chosen," *Boston Magazine*, June 1985, p. 192.

"I Gave Birth to My Sister's Baby," *Redbook*, April 1986, p. 34.

"Motherhood minus Mom," *Time*, 28 April 1986, p. 39.

"Natural Instincts Under Contract" *McLean's*, vol. 100, 23 March 1987, p. 13.

"Surrogate-gate," *Commonwealth*, vol. 114, 30 January 1987, p. 35.

"The Vatican Weighs In," *Science*, 20 March 1987, p. 1455.

"The Waiting Room: Scenes from a Surrogate Counseling Room" *California Magazine*, October 1983, p. 96.

Index

Abraham, Lorraine A., 89, 94, 103
Adoption, difficulty of, 18–19
Agencies, surrogate, mother services, 49–50
Amniocentesis, 17
Anthony, Pat, 25–26
Artificial insemination by donor (AID), 23
    legal aspects, 32–33
    process of, 23
    success rate, 23

Baby M case, 81–116
    appeal by Whitehead, 114
    class issue, 89–90
    contract in, 82
    effect on other surrogates, 62
    effects on child, 116
    Florida, Whitehead's flight to, 87–88
    guardian's recommendation, 103
    post-birth experience of Whitehead, 86–87
    pre-birth relationship, Sterns/Whitehead, 82–83, 85–86
    trial, 89–103
        summations, 104–108
    verdict, 111–113
    Whitehead's vistation, 88, 114–115, 116

Brodzinsky, Dr. David M., 95, 99
Brown, Louise, 21

Caplan, Dr. Arthur, 72
Capron, Alexander Morgan, 31
Cassidy, Harold J., 89, 92, 96, 107, 111
Contracts
    and surrogacy, 29–30, 38–39, 47
    Whitehead case, 82, 115–116

Dotterer, Maria, 63

Egg donation, 28
    process of, 28
Embryo transfer
    case of, 25–26
    process of, 24
    surrogate embryo transfer, 26–28
Ethical issues, 71–72
    creation of women breeders, 74–75
    guidelines for doctors, 71–72
    issues affecting couples/surrogates, 72–74
    issues affecting surrogate/her family, 74–75
    issues affecting unborn baby, 75–76

Family members, as surrogates, 25–26, 56–60
Fitzpatrick, Richard, 52
Freed, Dr. Doris Jonas, 32, 75
Frozen embryos, legal aspects, 35–37

Gardner, Richard A., 116
Genetic problems, and remaining childless, 16–17
Gore, Albert, 52
Graham, Robert, 68, 70

Handel, William, 49
Hergenhan, Susan, 101–102
Holder, Angela R., 116

Infertility, 14–28
    emotional issues of, 14–16
    options to artificial insemination by donor (AID), 23
    egg donation, 28
    embryo transfer, 24–28
    in vitro fertilization, 19–23
    surrogate embryo transfer, 26–28
    RESOLVE, self-help group, 15
In vitro fertilizaton, 19–23
    costs of, 22

In vitro *(continued)*
   good candidates for, 21
   legal aspects, 33–35
   process of, 19–21
   success rate, 22
Iradwanska, Ewa, 80

Keane, Noel P., 9, 12, 82
King, Sherry, 56–59

Legal aspects, 29–52
   of artificial insemination by donor (AID), 32–33, 44
   bans on surrogacy, 31
   and frozen embryos, 35–37
   of in vitro fertilization, 33–35
   proposed legislation, 117–118
   state regulation suggested legislation, 47–49, 50, 51–52
   surrogate mothers, 29–30, 37–52
      contracts, 29–30, 38–39, 47, 115–116
      couple rejects child, 42–43
      legal rights of child, 37
      surrogate as injured/wronged party, 45–46

McCormick, Rev. Richard A., 78
McKnight, Becky, 55
Malahoff, Alexander, 39–42
Mills, Karen, 59–60
Munoz, Alejandra, 63

Navarro-Valls, Joaquin, 77
Neal, Anne, 80
Nickman, Dr. Steven L., 101

O'Donnell, Edward J., 89

Parker, Philip J., 34
Parpalaix, Corinne, 33, 35
Pressler, Peggy, 64, 66
Prettyman, W. Marshall, 47

Religious issues
   defying God's will, 76
   Vatican, on extraordinary conception methods, 76–80
Repository for Germinal Science, 68, 70
RESOLVE, self-help group, 15
Rios, Mario and Elsa, 35–36

Salk, Dr. Lee, 93–94
Schechter, Dr. Marshall D., 94
Shinn, Rev. Roger, 70

Silverman, Phyllis R., 101
Skoloff, Gary M., 90, 92, 103, 107
Snyder, Deborah, 56
Sokoloff, Dr. Burton Z., 101
Sorkow, Judge Harvey R., 88, 108, 111–113
Sperm banks, 68, 70
State regulation of surrogate mothers, 47–49, 50, 51–52
Stern, Dr. Elizabeth/William. *See* Baby M case
Stiver, Judy, 39–42
Surrogate embryo transfer, 26–28
    process of, 26
Surrogate mothers, 24–28
    agencies for, 49–50
    as business, 71
    costs of, 49, 73
    and creation of women breeders, 74–75
    earliest case, 9–12
    embryo transfer, 24–28
    ethical issues, 67–76, 71–72
    experiences of
        negative experiences, 62
        positive experiences, 54–60
    family members as, 56–60
    historical view, 54
    legal aspects, 29–30, 37–52
    opponents of, 68, 70–71
    private arrangements, 51
    reasons for use of, 72–73
    reasons for volunteering, 54
    religious issues, 76–80
    role of, 9, 24, 53
    study of, 54
    surrogate embryo transfer, 26–28
    surrogates/clients relationship between, 61–62
    visitation rights of, 64, 66–67
    See also specific topics.

Tay-Sachs disease, 17

Vatican, on extraordinary conception methods, 76–80
Visitation rights, of surrogate mothers, 64, 66–67

Whitehead, Mary Beth
    background information, 85
    See also Baby M case.
Williams, Carolyn, 54